By Hywel John

Cast in alphabetical order

Beatrice	**Louise Collins**
Sophie	**Lisa Jackson**
Jack	**Steven Meo**

Director	**Kate Wasserberg**
Designer	**Mark Bailey**
Lighting	**Tom White**
Sound	**Andrea J Cox**

Company Stage Manager	**Hazel Price**
Deputy Stage Manager	**Nicola Ireland**
Assistant Stage Manager	**Tracey Booth**

First performed at Clwyd Theatr Cymru
Thursday 22 April - Saturday 15 May 2010
Dydd Iau 22 Ebrill - Dydd Sadwrn 15 Mai 2010

"Some of the most consistently exciting ensemble theatre in Britain is currently being produced by Hands' Clwyd company."
***** The Guardian

Created through the vision of Clwyd County Council and its Chief Executive Haydn Rees, Theatr Clwyd was opened in 1976. Located a mile from Mold town centre, the building incorporates five performance venues: the Anthony Hopkins Theatre, Emlyn Williams Theatre, Studio 2, multi-function Clwyd Room for the community, cinema and three art galleries.

Following local government reorganisation in Wales, the theatre faced closure on 1st April 1997. The new Flintshire County Council and its leader, Tom Middlehurst, asked Terry Hands to formulate an artistic and business plan to avert this threat and take the theatre forward.

Terry Hands accepted the post of Director on 2 May 1997 and asked Tim Baker to join him as Associate.

In 1998, the theatre won the Barclays/TMA Theatre of the Year Award and, in 1999, was designated a Welsh National Performing Arts Company by the Arts Council of Wales. The name was changed to Clwyd Theatr Cymru to reflect the theatre's new national remit and its new Welsh identity.

Subsequently, the theatre has become the most productive national performing arts company in Wales.

President/Llywydd Lord Kinnock
Chairman/Cadeirydd Hilary Isherwood
Director/Cyfarwyddwr Terry Hands

ASSOCIATES/AELODAU CYSWLLT

Simon Armstrong	Bradley Freegard	Jenny Livsey	Christian Patterson
Robert Blythe	Sara Harris-Davies	Steven Meo	Robert Perkins
Philip Bretherton	Daniel Hawksford	Dyfrig Morris	Victoria Pugh
Alun ap Brinley	Lynn Hunter	Siwan Morris	Steffan Rhodri
John Cording	Lee Haven Jones	Simon Nehan	Oliver Ryan
Ifan Huw Dafydd	Julian Lewis Jones	Kai Owen	Owen Teale
Steven Elliott	Gwyn Vaughan Jones	Vivien Parry	Johnson Willis

DIRECTORS CYFARWYDDWYR	**DESIGNERS** CYNLLUNWYR	**WRITERS** YSGRIFENWYR	**COMPOSERS** CYFANSODDWYR
Tim Baker	Mark Bailey	Meredydd Barker	Dyfan Jones
Terry Hands	Martyn Bainbridge	Manon Eames	Colin Towns
Peter Rowe	Nick Beadle		
	Max Jones		
	Timothy O'Brien		

Louise Collins

Louise was born in Bridgend and trained at RADA.

Previous productions at Clwyd Theatr Cymru include: Poppy in **Noises Off** directed by Terry Hands, Mary in **The Suicide**, Mariana in **Measure for Measure**, directed by Phillip Breen, Hermia in **A Midsummer Night's Dream**, directed by Tim Baker and Abigail in **The Crucible**, directed by Terry Hands.

Other credits include: Joan in **St Joan** by George Bernard Shaw at the Fisher Center, New York and toured Wisconsin and Illinois with **The Tempest**, in which she played Miranda and Ariel, directed by Gregory Thompson for AandBC Theatre Company; Juliet in **Romeo and Juliet**, directed by Ellie Jones at the New Wolsey Theatre; Kitty in **Anna Kareina** at the Royal Lyceum, directed by Muriel Romanus; Bethan in **The Pull of Negative Gravity** by Jonathan Lichtenstein, which won a Fringe First at the Traverse Theatre and at 59e59 Theaters, New York for the Brits Off Broadway Festival; Meg in **Amazed and Confused**, directed by Fiona Weir at the Royal Court, The Ghost of Christmas Past in **A Christmas Carol** at Southwark Playhouse, directed by Ellie Jones, and Electra in **The Oresteia**, Ted Hughes' adaptation, directed by Gregory Thompson at the Fisher Center, New York.

Film and television credits: Rhiannon in **Nice Day for a Welsh Wedding**, **Belonging** (BBC Wales); **A Night on the Tiles** (ITV Wales); **Home** (Forget About It TV and Films).

Radio: **Doctor Who** (Big Finish Productions); **The White People** (Radio 7); Ellie in **Out of the Ordinary** by Gary Owen for Radio 4.

Lisa Jackson

Lisa trained at the London Academy of Music and Dramatic Art and **Pieces** is her first role for Clwyd Theatr Cymru.

Lisa's theatre credits include: **All My Sons** (Curve Theatre, Leicester); **Time and the Conways** (Royal National Theatre); **As You Like It** (Watford Palace Theatre); **The 39 Steps** (West Yorkshire Playhouse); **Major Barbara** (Royal Exchange); **Meteorite** (Hampstead Theatre); **Black 'Ell** (Soho Theatre).

Television credits include: **Campus** (Channel 4); **Waking the Dead** (BBC); **The Marchioness Disaster** (YTV); **Daniel Deronda** (BBC).

Film credits: Mary Mouse in **Bright Young Things**, written and directed by Stephen Fry.

Steven Meo

Steven was born and bred in Coelbren at the top of the Swansea Valley. He graduated from the Royal Welsh College of Music and Drama in 1999 and is a proud associate artist of Clwyd Theatr Cymru.

Steven's theatre credits include: **Arden of Faversham, Great Expectations, Under Milk Wood, Portrait of the Artist As a Young Dog**, and **Dealer's Choice** (all for Clwyd Theatr Cymru); **Woyzeck** (Wyeside Theatre); **East From the Gantry** (Edinburgh Festival); **Metamorphosis** (Merlin Theatre, Budapest); **Up 'n' Under** (Bristol Old Vic); **Amgen: Broken, Flesh and Blood** (both for Sherman Cymru); **Crazy Gary's Mobile Disco** (Paines Plough/Lyric Hammersmith); **Beautiful Thing** (Sound Theatre) and **The Caucasian Chalk Circle** (Shared Experience and West Yorkshire Playhouse).

TV and film credits include: **Nice Girl** (BBC2); **Without Motive** (ITV); **Score** (BBC); **Belonging** (BBC Wales); **Holby City** (BBC1); **High Hopes** (BBC Wales); **Roger Roger** (BBC1); **Innovations** (BBC Wales); **The Trouble With George** (BBC1); **Doctors** (BBC1); **Spine Chillers** (BBC3); **Torchwood** (BBC2); **Grownups** (BBC3); **Casualty** (BBC1); **Uncle Mike** (BBC); **Good Arrows** (Dust Films/ITV); **Gavin and Stacey** (BBC1) and **Doctor Who: The Infinite Quest** (animated series).

Radio credits include: **Honey, The Harbour, The Owl Service, Fallen, Afterlife, Cube of the Rainbow, Taking Leave, In Parenthesis**, and the digital remake of **Under Milk Wood**.

Hywel John
Writer

Pieces is Hywel's first play.

He is also an actor and trained at LAMDA. Recent theatre credits include: **Salome** (Headlong, Tour and Hampstead Theatre); **The Glass Menagerie** (Clwyd Theatr Cymru); **A Stab in the Dark** (Latitude Festival); **Macbeth** (Chichester, West End and Broadway); **Angry Young Man** (Trafalgar Studios, Adelaide Festival, BAC, Edinburgh Festival) and **Twelfth Night** (Chichester).

Film and TV credits include: **Macbeth** (BBC Films, PBS America and Illuminations); **The IT Crowd** (Channel 4) and **Doctors** (BBC).

Hywel co-runs the award-winning MahWaff Theatre Company (www.mahwaff.com).

Kate Wasserberg

Director

Kate is New Plays Director at Clwyd Theatr Cymru where she has directed **The Glass Menagerie** (CTC and tour) and **A History of Falling Things** by James Graham (CTC and the Sherman Theatre, Cardiff). Kate was Artistic Director of the **Write to Rock** project (CTC) and the Assistant Director on **Noises Off** and **Arden of Faversham**.

Previous to this, she was Associate Director of the Finborough Theatre, London, where she directed: **Sons of York** and **Little Madam**, both by James Graham, and **The Representative**, **I Wish to Die Singing** and **The New Morality**. Kate will direct **The Man** by James Graham at the Finborough Theatre this spring.

Other directing includes: 2007 Schools Festival (Young Vic); **Switzerland** (HighTide Festival); **Doing Lines** (Pleasance); **Blue Velvet** (Gilded Balloon); **The Studio** (south-west tour) and **The Firebird** (Exeter Phoenix).

As an assistant director, Kate has worked at the Barbican, the Abbey Theatre, Dublin; the Young Vic, Shakespeare's Globe and the Theatre Royal Bath.

Mark Bailey

Designer

Mark Bailey has designed over 150 productions in Britain, Europe and North America.

He is an associate artist of Clwyd Theatr Cymru where his many designs include: **Shakespeare's Will**, **To Kill a Mockingbird**, **Pygmalion**, **The Glass Menagerie**, **A History of Falling Things**, **Noises Off**, **Great Expectations**, **The Suicide**, **A Midsummer Night's Dream**, **An Ideal Husband**, **Of Mice and Men**, **The Way It Was**, **Present Laughter**, **A Chorus of Disapproval**, **The Druid's Rest**, **Hobson's Choice**, **Brassed Off**, **Hay Fever**, **Waiting for Godot**, **One Flew Over the Cuckoo's Nest**, **Pleasure and Repentance**, **Accidental Death of an Anarchist**, **Hard Times**, **Portrait of the Artist As a Young Dog**, **Oleanna**, **A View From the Bridge**, **Blithe Spirit**, **Oh What a Lovely War**, **The Four Seasons**, **Silas Marner**, **Betrayal**, **The Rabbit**, **King Lear**, **Private Lives** and the Alexander Cordell trilogy: **Rape of the Fair Country**, **Hosts of Rebecca** and **Song of the Earth**.

Recent designs include: **The Snow Queen** for English National Ballet; **Macbeth** for the Chicago Shakespeare Theatre; **Privates on Parade** at the West Yorkshire Playhouse, and in the West End; **Legal Fictions** (Savoy); **Rent** at the

Duke of York's, and set for **The Rise and Fall of the City of Mahagonny** for Los Angeles Opera. Other work includes: **Hamlet** (Chicago Shakespeare Theatre); national tours of **The Rivals** and **Mack and Mabel** (also in the West End); **To Reach the Clouds** (Nottingham Playhouse); **The Importance of Being Earnest** (Oxford Playhouse); **The Threepenny Opera** (National Theatre and tour); **Rat Pack Confidential** (West End/Nottingham Playhouse); **The Resistible Rise of Arturo Ui** (Glasgow Citzens).

Designs for music and dance include: **Melody on the Move** (English National Ballet); **Iolanthe** (Savoy); **Ariadne auf Naxos** (Maggio Musicale Florence and Opera de Lausanne); **Il Maestro di Cappella**, **Susanna's Secret** and **The Telephone** (Buxton Festival); **Carmen** (ROH Linbury Studio); **Ladders and Snakes** (Opera North); **False Love/True Love** and **What Price Confidence?** (Almeida Opera). He has also designed **Into the Woods** (Theatre Royal York); **Cabaret, Irma la Douce, Fiddler on the Roof** and **The Gondoliers** (also West End), all for the Watermill, Newbury, all of which won or were nominated for TMA Best Musical Awards.

Other work in London includes: national tours of: **Entertaining Mr Sloane** (Greenwich); **Peace in Our Time, A Chorus of Disapproval** and **Hadrian VII** (Richmond); **The Importance of Being Earnest** (Old Vic/Toronto); **The Winslow Boy** (Gielgud); **A Judgement in Stone**

(Lyric Hammersmith); costumes for **Which Witch** (Piccadilly) and **Present Laughter** (Aldwych and Wyndham's).

Future productions include: **Madama Butterfly** for Nevill Holt and Grange Park opera festivals and **Sleeping Beauty** for Hong Kong Ballet.

Mark has also designed **Broken Lives** for BBC Television.

Tom White

Lighting Designer

Tom graduated from the technical theatre arts course at Middlesex University in 2004 and now lights a variety of productions, ranging from medium-scale UK tours to international musicals and operettas. His work has been seen in Egypt, Italy, Romania, Austria, Spain and France. He works regularly with Tangled Feet (Stage Award and Fringe First nominees 2007/8), the Roundhouse Theatre Company and Proyecto Opera (based in Valladolid, Spain).

Tom's other production role credits include: **BBC Electric Proms**, **Paris Autoshow 2008**, Longborough Festival Opera, **Whipping It Up** (West End and UK tour); the Roundhouse, the Wrestling School Company, the Gate Theatre, London; the Bush Theatre and Paines Plough.

Recent theatre credits: **Dry Sigh** (Resolution, the Place); **Madness in Valencia** (Trafalgar Studios); **The Glass Menagerie** (Clwyd Theatr Cymru and Welsh national tour); **A History of Falling Things** (Clwyd Theatr Cymru); **Where's My Desi Soulmate?** (Theatre Royal Stratford East and tour); **Sons of York** (Finborough Theatre); **The Halo Project** (Bush Theatre); **50 Ways to Leave Your Lover** (Bush Theatre); **The Pink Bedroom** (Courtyard Theatre); **Weapons of Happiness** (Finborough Theatre); **Little Madam** (Finborough Theatre); **Poofloose With Stephen De Martin, One Poof and a Piano** (Udderbelly); **Game?** by Tangled Feet (Theatre503, then UK tour); **Hedda Gabler** (Teatrul Bulandra in Bucharest, Romania); **Love Child** (Finborough Theatre); **Mozart's Back** (Assembly Rooms); **Emily's Kitchen** (Gilded Balloon); **The Representative** (Finborough Theatre); **Hamlet and Malvolio and His Masters** (Southwark Playhouse); **Deir Yassan Day** (Bloomsbury Theatre); **Yesterday Was a Weird Day** (BAC); **Cargo** (Northern School of Contemporary Dance); **Catching Dust** by Tangled Feet (Teatro Della Contraddizione, Milan, Italy); **Miss Julie** (Greenwich Playhouse); **Snapshots** and **Maybe Baby** (Old Red Lion Theatre); **A Servant of Two Masters** (New End Theatre, Hampstead); **Sotoba Komachi** and **The Damask Drum** (Greenwich Playhouse).

Opera credits include: **La bohème** (Longborough Festival Opera); **The Pearl Fishers** (Feria De Valladolid); **The Marriage of Figaro** (UK tour); **Simon Boccanegra** (Feria de Valladolid, Spain); **The Immortal Orchestra in Concert** (the Roundhouse in Camden); **The Crocodile** (Arcola Theatre as part of the Grimeborn season).

Musical credits: Stacey Solomon **X Factor** homecoming concert (Freemantle Media); **Dick Whittington** (Broadway Theatre, Barking); **Sleeping Beauty** (Broadway Theatre, Barking); **Alyona** (Theatre am Lend, Graz, Austria); Shola Ama and special guests in concert (Roundhouse).

Andrea J Cox
Sound Designer

Andrea studied Physics and Philosophy at Liverpool University. She has designed shows and worked for the Liverpool Everyman, Bristol Old Vic and extensively for the Royal Shakespeare Company.

Sound designs include:
For the RSC in the Courtyard Theatre, Stratford on Avon and at the Roundhouse in London – **The Histories** (all 8 plays from **Richard II** to **Henry V**).

In the Royal Shakespeare Theatre: **Twelfth Night** (Adrian Noble), **The Winter's Tale, Antony and Cleopatra, Measure for Measure** (Sean Holmes), **Macbeth, Hamlet, Twelfth Night** (Michael Boyd), **The Comedy of Errors** (also in the West End and on Tour).

In the Swan Theatre: **The Silent Woman, The Duchess of Malfi, Troilus and Cressida, 'Tis Pity She's a Whore, The Theban Plays, A Jovial Crew, Elgar's Rondo, The Broken Heart, The Devil Is an Ass, Three Hours After Marriage, Little Eyolf, Tales From Ovid** (also at the Young Vic); **Henry VI** parts 1, 2 and 3 and **Richard III** (also at the Power Centre, Michigan USA and the Young Vic); **Love in a Wood, As You Like It** (also at the Kennedy Center, Washington DC).

At The Other Place: **Measure for Measure** (Trevor Nunn), **Ghosts, Henry VI** (Katie Mitchell), **The Phoenician Women, The Mysteries, Shadows, Bad Weather, A Warwickshire Testimony, The Servant of Two Masters** (also at the Young Vic and in the West End); **Richard II, La Lupa, Back to Methuselah, Desire Under the Elms**.

RSC New Work Festivals 2004/05: in the Swan Theatre & Arts Theatre – **Tynan**; at the Soho Theatre – **Postcards from America** (**Eric La Rue** & **Elective Affinities**).

Other designs: **The Pull of Negative Gravity** at the Mercury Theatre, Colchester, also at the Edinburgh Traverse and 59E59 in New York; **Sons of York** at the Finborough Theatre; **The Scarecrow and His Servant** at Southwark Playhouse; **The Oresteia** trilogy at the Fisher Center, Bard College, New York; **A Christmas Carol, A Doll's House** at Bridge House Theatre, **The Clink** for Birmingham School of Acting at the Crescent Theatre.

CLWYD THEATR CYMRU

PRESIDENT Lord Kinnock | **CHAIRMAN** Cllr Hilary Isherwood | **DIRECTOR** Terry Hands

CLWYD THEATR CYMRU BOARD OF GOVERNORS

Fiona Allan
Cllr Chris Bithell
David Brierley
Simon Carter
Cllr Carolyn Cattermoul
Cllr Ron Davies
Keith Evans
Colin Everett
Cllr Robin Guest
Cllr George Hardcastle
Cllr Patrick Heesom
Cllr Hilary Isherwood
Cllr Peter Macfarlane
Prof Michael Scott
Geraint Stanley Jones
Cllr Helen Yale

CLWYD THEATR CYMRU COMPANY

Catrin Aaron
Sherry Baines
Robert Blythe
Louise Collins
Richard Elfyn
Karen Ford
Michael Geary
Charlotte Gray
James Haggie
Tony Haygarth
Lisa Jackson
Olivia Mace
Steven Meo
Dyfrig Morris
Francois Pandolfo
Sion Pritchard
Lucy Rivers
Hilary Tones
Llion Williams

ASSOCIATE DIRECTOR
Tim Baker

GENERAL MANAGER
Julia Grime

ASSOCIATE DIRECTOR:
PLAYS & TOURING
William James

DIRECTOR: NEW PLAYS
Kate Wasserberg

CASTING
Leigh-Ann Regan

PA TO THE DIRECTORS
Melanie Jones

ASSISTANT TO GENERAL MANAGER
William McMillan

EDUCATION

EDUCATION PRODUCER
Anne Plenderleith

EDUCATION ADMINISTRATOR
Nerys Edwards

EDUCATION CO-ORDINATOR
Jane Meakin

DRAMA OUTREACH WORKER
Emyr John

TUTORS
Carolyn Davies-Moore,
Clare-Louise Edwards,
Claire Howard, Zoë
Knapman, Jenny
Stockbridge, Laura Welsby

FINANCE

FINANCIAL MANAGER
Emma Sullivan

FINANCE ASSISTANTS
Sandra Almeida, Carol
Parsonage

GALLERIES

GALLERY CURATOR
Jonathan Le Vay

MARKETING

MARKETING MANAGER
Ann Williams

SPONSORSHIP MANAGER
Annie Dayson

BOX OFFICE MANAGER
Marie Thorpe

PRESS OFFICER
Anthony Timothy

DEPUTY MARKETING MANAGER
Morwenna Honan

MARKETING ASSISTANT
Angharad Madog

DISTRIBUTION
Brian Swarbrick

BOX OFFICE ASSISTANTS
Carol Edwards, Rosemary
Hughes, Nikki Jones, Jan
Lewis, Fiona Powell, Jean
Proctor, Mair Eluned Rush,
Jennifer Walters, Mary
Williams

PRODUCTION

PRODUCTION MANAGER
Jim Davis

DEPUTY PRODUCTION MANAGER
Hannah Lobb

TECHNICAL & DEVELOPMENT MANAGER
Pat Nelder

TECHNICAL STAGE MANAGER
Jayson Noble

DEPUTY TECHNICAL STAGE MANAGER
Paul Adams

ASSISTANT TECHNICAL STAGE MANAGERS
Angel Hasted, Scott
Howard, Nic Samuel

HEAD OF WARDROBE
Deborah Knight

WARDROBE CUTTERS
Emma Aldridge, Michal
Shyne

WARDROBE ASSISTANT
Alison Hartnell

COSTUME MAINTENANCE
Cath Jones, Amber Smit

HEAD OF LX & SOUND
Keith Hemming

DEPUTY HEAD LX & SOUND
Kevin Heyes

DEPUTY (LIGHTING)
Geoff Farmer

ASSISTANT ELECTRICIANS
Dan Armishaw, Gareth
Hughes, Matthew
Williams, Neil Williams

PROPERTIES
Eugenie Hardstone

PROPERTIES CARPENTER
Bob Heaton

HEAD OF WORKSHOP
John Wynne-Eyton

CONSTRUCTION
Steve Eccleson, Tom
Parsons, Andy Sutters

SCENIC ARTIST
Mike Jones

WIG MISTRESS
Louise Penman

THEATRE MANAGEMENT

THEATRE MANAGER
Kenneth Anthonisz

BUILDING SERVICES MANAGER
Jim Scarratt

HOUSE MANAGER
Marion Wright

ASSISTANT FRONT OF HOUSE MANAGERS
Maivena Bingham,
Elena Vedovotto

SHOP MANAGER
Wendy Dawson

RECEPTIONISTS/ BOOKSHOP
Carole Adams, Emma
Brunt, Sandra Fletcher,
Elaine Godwin, Carole
Jones, Nerys Jones,
Jennifer Walters

CLEANING SUPERVISOR
Mark Sandham

CLEANERS
Tracey D'Amato, Lorraine
Jones, Maxine Kalewski,
Tara Pritchard, Ann Shaw,
Patricia Williams, Richard
Williams

SALES ASSISTANTS
Liz Gamble, Elaine Jones,
Luisa Sciarillo, Emily
Thelwell, Christine Wright

BAR MANAGER
Salv Vena

RESTAURANT MANAGER
Rhian Walls

DEPUTY RESTAURANT MANAGER
Nicola Wyatt

PROJECTIONISTS
Mike Batchelor
Mike Roberts
Matthew Wright

STAGE MANAGEMENT

COMPANY STAGE MANAGERS
Helen Drew, Hazel Price,
Bryony Rutter (TYP)

STAGE MANAGER
(on the book)
Edward Salt

DEPUTY STAGE MANAGER
Nicola Ireland

ASSISTANT STAGE MANAGER
Tracey Booth

ADDITIONAL STAFF FOR *PIECES*

WARDROBE SUPERVISOR
Fi Carrington

DRESSER
Gillian Brockley

SCENIC ARTIST
Katy Salt

WIGS, HAIR AND MAKE UP SUPERVISOR
Deb Kenton

PRODUCTION PHOTOGRAPHY
Catherine Ashmore

CREDITS FOR *PIECES*

British Heart Foundation
Cascade Designer Cakes
Help the Aged

PIECES

Hywel John

For Amy and those she left behind

A simple child,
That lightly draws its breath,
And feels its life in every limb,
What should it know of death?

William Wordsworth, *We Are Seven*

Let Love clasp Grief lest both be drowned

Alfred, Lord Tennyson, *In Memoriam* (*1*)

Behold, we know not anything;
I can but trust that good shall fall
At last – far off – at last, to all,
And every winter change to spring.

So runs my dream; but what am I?
An infant crying in the night;
An infant crying for the light,
And with no language but a cry.

Alfred, Lord Tennyson, *In Memoriam* (*54*)

Characters

SOPHIE, *mid-thirties, godmother to Bea and Jack*
JACK, *twin brother to Bea*
BEA, *twin sister to Jack*

Jack and Bea are children, but must be played by adults.

Notes on the Text

–   *indicates an interruption by the following line.*

...   *indicates an ellipsis / an hiatus / a pause, the length*
           and quality of which to be determined in rehearsal and
           performance. More often than not, silent, but not
           necessarily still, and never empty.

/   *indicates an overlap: the moment where the following*
           line (spoken by another character) should start.

The dialogue should be explored for other potential overlaps
that are not otherwise stated with a /, particularly with dialogue
between the twins, as long as the sense of the lines is retained.

This text went to press before the end of rehearsals and so may
differ slightly from the play as performed.

Scene One

Summer. Dusk.

The large lounge of a family house set remotely alone in the countryside.

There are curtained French windows that open out onto a garden, which backs onto the edge of a large forest. The curtains are open.

On the other side of the room a door leads to the front door and the rest of the house.

It is furnished simply and comfortably: definitely a sofa, perhaps armchairs, a coffee table, or even a floor cushion or two. There is a small reading lamp and a telephone.

The room reflects the house's most recent inhabitants: a youngish married couple with two children, a boy and a girl; it is filled with the assorted paraphernalia of family life – mementos, memorabilia, etc.

There are a variety of family photos on display: photos of both the parents and the children should be posed by the actors playing the children.

There are books everywhere, piled up and packed into shelves: fiction, poetry, plays, lots of children's material, and all sorts of non-fiction (encyclopaedias, reference books, magazines, etc.).

It is a comfy, friendly-feeling room – chaotic, well kept, but with enough space for plenty of movement.

There is no clock in the room.

There is a television. It is off.

SOPHIE, JACK *and* BEA *enter. They are all dressed smartly in black; the reason for which becomes apparent.*

No one speaks for a short time.

JACK *and* BEA *sit down.*

SOPHIE. Well… here we are.

>Do you want to go and get changed?

>You look so handsome in that suit, Jack. And you look lovely, Beatrice, lovely…

BEA. I hate black.

JACK. You've got loads of black.

BEA. Well, I don't like this black, Jack.

JACK. Black's black, Bea.

BEA. You're in black too, idiot.

SOPHIE. Beatrice –

JACK. I like black stuff.

BEA. You look like you're going to school.

JACK. Shut up.

SOPHIE. Jack –

>JACK *and* BEA *laugh*.

>…

>What about some food? Are you hungry?

JACK. I've had lots, thanks.

BEA. You stuffed your face.

JACK. I had about fifty sausage rolls.

SOPHIE. Of course, silly me –

BEA. Mum'll call you a greedy pig.

JACK. I am a greedy pig.

SOPHIE. How about a drink or something…?

JACK. Are you going to live with us now?

>…

BEA. Mum and Dad told us once that –

JACK. Your godparents have to look after you, and that's the law.

SOPHIE. Jack. Beatrice –

JACK. Mum and Dad don't have any brothers or sisters –

BEA. We don't have any cousins, do you?

...

SOPHIE. Well –

JACK. And also our grannies and stuff are dead –

BEA. We never met anyone else.

JACK. Mum and Dad told us that we were the first twins ever –

BEA. In our families –

JACK. Ever.

SOPHIE. Yes, I remember, I know.

JACK. Maybe we have some fourth cousins a million times removed or something –

BEA. But that doesn't count.

SOPHIE. No, I suppose it doesn't.

...

BEA. I remember you from ages ago.

JACK. Where have you been?

SOPHIE. Well, I've sent you both birthday and Christmas cards, haven't I? And postcards?

JACK. Yes, we know where you live, but how come you haven't visited us?

BEA. You're our godmum.

SOPHIE. I know, of course, and I'm sorry, but it's, well, there's lots of boring reasons...

I have been thinking about you all the time.

JACK. You're here now.

SOPHIE. Yes, I'm here now.

You were so little last time I came.

JACK. I don't really remember you.

BEA. Don't be stupid, I remember so you must remember.

JACK. No, not really.

SOPHIE. Oh, well, that's a shame.

JACK. I mean, you're quite familiar.

BEA. It was at our birthday party, I don't know which one, but it was definitely at our birthday party –

SOPHIE. Yes, it was. You were very little though.

JACK. Which one was it?

BEA. I don't know, do I?

JACK. We must have been small for me not to remember.

BEA. Well, I remember. (*To* SOPHIE.) I just kind of remember you. You were there.

JACK. Oh, that's helpful.

BEA. Shut up.

Also, Mum and Dad shouted.

JACK. I don't remember that at all. They never shout.

BEA. They do.

SOPHIE. Yes, yes, well, everyone has to have a shout sometimes.

...

SOPHIE *turns to go, but as soon as her back is turned* JACK *and* BEA *briefly shout loudly, stopping abruptly.*

JACK *and* BEA *laugh.*

...

You're both still mischievous, I see.

JACK. Are you going to look after us?

SOPHIE. Yes.

BEA. You're our godmum.

SOPHIE. Yes, but I'm called Sophie, remember?

Scene Two

The next morning. Early.

The curtains are drawn. Only the lamp is on.

JACK *and* BEA *are reading. There are all sorts of books strewn about.*

They are still dressed in yesterday's clothes.

SOPHIE *enters, still wearing the same skirt from yesterday.*

SOPHIE. Good morning.

SOPHIE *goes to open the curtains.*

You're up very early.

JACK *and* BEA. Good morning.

Warm, early-morning sunlight pours into the room.

SOPHIE. Oh!

JACK. What?

BEA. What's the matter?

SOPHIE. You're both still wearing your... did you sleep in them?

BEA. No.

...

SOPHIE. I'm a little lost.

BEA. We read it.

SOPHIE. Read what?

BEA. We're in the mourning, see?

SOPHIE. Yes, I see…

Well, no, I don't see. What on earth have you been up to?

SOPHIE *starts to clear up some of the books*.

BEA. It's an ancient custom, isn't it?

SOPHIE. What is?

JACK. To wear black when you are in the mourning.

SOPHIE. I see, yes, of course.

BEA. 'Black is worn until the mourning finishes –'

JACK. And we are in the mourning for Mum and Dad.

BEA. You're still wearing your black skirt.

JACK. She's only half in the mourning.

SOPHIE. I don't have all of my clothes with me yet.

…

Are you hungry? Shall I whip up some breakfast?

JACK. In some countries people don't eat when they mourn.

SOPHIE. But not in this country. You must be hungry.

BEA. Not really.

SOPHIE. Surely you'll eat something.

JACK. We don't feel very hungry.

BEA. Jack's still full of sausage rolls.

JACK. I'm a greedy pig.

SOPHIE. Not if you don't eat you're not!

JACK. Yes.

…

SOPHIE. So what do you two want to do today?

BEA. We don't know.

SOPHIE. Would you like to see some friends?

JACK. No, I don't think so.

SOPHIE. Perhaps we could do something together?

Maybe we could go for a walk?

In the woods? I remember your mum used to love...

BEA. It's weird, Sophie.

SOPHIE. What is, Beatrice?

BEA. You... here.

SOPHIE. I'm sure it is.

BEA. Not weird bad, just... weird.

JACK. I think what Bea is trying to say is that she misses Mum and Dad.

BEA. I didn't say that!

JACK. But that's what you meant underneath.

BEA. Who cares about underneath? / I'm not underneath anything!

SOPHIE. Children, please. Beatrice.

JACK. Sorry, Bea.

BEA. It's okay.

...

SOPHIE. Look. I'm sure it feels weird for both of you. Hopefully not... not weird bad.

You haven't seen me for a long time, so I, I understand.

It feels, well, weird for me too. But I'm also happy... happy to see you both.

BEA. I'm happy to see you this morning.

SOPHIE. I'm glad.

BEA. I'm sure Jack is too.

JACK. Yes, that's right.

...

Did you know, in some countries, people in the mourning never leave their home until the mourning finishes?

Scene Three

Later the same day. Early afternoon.

Outside, a sudden heavy downpour is coming to an end.
Eventually the clouds pass, to be replaced by bright sunlight.

SOPHIE *enters, with a shopping bag. She is still in the same*
black skirt as the previous scene. She is soaking wet.

JACK *and* BEA *are dressed as before. They are sitting next to*
each other. More books are strewn about. If anything, the room
might be messier than before.

SOPHIE. I'm sorry I took so long. Have you managed without
me?

I got a bit lost. Twice. In town and on my way back. I forgot
how far away we are. It's silly, I know – I mean, I think
yesterday I just didn't notice – I wasn't thinking about it.

The bus driver dropped me off and I couldn't for the life of
me make head or tail of where I was. It took me half an hour
to get home from the bus stop and then I got caught in the…

But I've got myself some clothes, for the next few days, until
my things arrive.

BEA. Let me see.

SOPHIE. Well… (*She gets a new skirt out of the bag.*) I bought
this. What do you think?

BEA. Um… it's pretty, but…

SOPHIE. What?

BEA. But not as pretty as you are.

SOPHIE. That's very sweet of you.

BEA. Actually… I don't think it's pretty.

SOPHIE. Oh really?

BEA. No, sorry, I was fibbing.

SOPHIE. Well, you shouldn't fib –

BEA. No, sorry, Sophie.

SOPHIE. What do you really think?

BEA. I think it's a bit boring.

SOPHIE. Oh.

BEA. Like what our teachers wear.

SOPHIE. Really?

BEA. I don't think you're boring.

SOPHIE. Well, I rather like it.

BEA. I like colourful things, don't you?

SOPHIE. I think… this will do just fine. What do you think, Jack?

JACK. Why are you asking me?

BEA. Sophie, listen, Jack knows *nothing* about fashion.

SOPHIE. I bet you have an opinion though, Jack.

BEA. I wouldn't bother.

JACK. I think I prefer your black skirt. The one you're wearing.

SOPHIE. Oh really, why's that?

JACK. I don't know –

BEA. I told you, don't bother.

SOPHIE. Perhaps I'll keep it on for today, for you, Jack, and tomorrow I'll wear the new one.

JACK. That sounds fair to me.

SOPHIE. Wonderful.

Now, I think it's lunchtime.

JACK *and* BEA. We've eaten.

SOPHIE. Oh really?

BEA. We had baked beans –

JACK. On toast.

SOPHIE. Is that all you want?

JACK. We're full up, thanks.

BEA. We ate just after you left, actually.

JACK. Obviously we did, otherwise she would have seen us, wouldn't she?

BEA. I got hungry starving and really wanted some baked beans on toast –

JACK. But I said no, no we can't, because in the mourning you can't eat, it's not allowed until it finishes –

BEA. Yeah, but actually that's stupid 'cos you have to eat something –

JACK. I got really hungry too, but then I read that –

BEA. No, I read it –

JACK. That in the mourning –

BEA. You eat fast.

SOPHIE. What?

JACK. No, you don't eat fast.

BEA. Yeah, you eat really fast.

JACK. No, that's not it, you get to eat, but only after you don't eat fast.

SOPHIE. Oh God, you mean you *fast*.

BEA. Yeah!

JACK. So obviously we've done that part of the mourning, we've finished that bit – we hadn't eaten since yesterday afternoon, and that's not very much time at all, so that's pretty fast.

BEA. Yeah, but that's not really why it's called not eating fast.

JACK. Yes, it is –

BEA. No, it's not –

JACK. I just said it was –

BEA. So what – ?

SOPHIE. So why is it?

JACK. I just said, because –

BEA. No! Let me say – we're not at school, it's my turn – it's because – oh, I think this is brilliant – because I think when the mourning finishes then you're really, really hungry and so you eat your elevenses at like a million miles an hour.

JACK. That's silly and you don't eat them that fast, not really.

BEA. Pretty much.

SOPHIE. Well, I'm glad you've eaten something.

BEA. And we've washed up our dishes – they're drying on the rack.

SOPHIE. Well…

Well done you.

BEA. Mum and Dad always say you should –

JACK *and* BEA. 'Do your own washing up.'

SOPHIE. You've been taught well, I see.

BEA. We have to remember everything they say to us, don't we?

SOPHIE. Yes, remembering them is very important.

BEA. I don't think we'll ever forget.

JACK. We'll never forget.

BEA. I know exactly how Mummy cleans the dishes. She always scrapes the leftovers into the bin –

JACK. Then rinses the plate, holding it with her left hand –

BEA. Before leaving it to soak a bit in the sink.

JACK. Then she scrubs it clean.

BEA. How do you do it?

SOPHIE. I don't know, I suppose I –

JACK. It doesn't matter, Sophie, because I think we'll do the washing-up in future.

SOPHIE. Why, Jack, that's a very kind offer, but I'm sure it will be my turn at some point.

BEA. Yeah, Jack, you can do it all if you like.

SOPHIE. And I thought your mum and dad said, 'Do your own washing-up.'

JACK. Oh yes, that's right.

...

Me and Bea will do it most of the time, just like Mum and Dad do it most of the time, then you can do it sometimes too, just like we only do it sometimes too.

SOPHIE. I'll tell you what, why don't we see what happens when we actually have a meal together?

BEA. That sounds fair to me.

JACK. That sounds fair to me.

SOPHIE. That... sounds fair to me too.

JACK *opens a book.* BEA *joins him and they start to read.*

Scene Four

Later in the day. Late afternoon, around teatime.

They are all dressed as before.

JACK *and* BEA *are still reading. Books are once again strewn about.*

SOPHIE *is standing as before.*

SOPHIE. I'm just thinking, thinking that now must be the time that normally you come home from school?

BEA *looks up from her book.* JACK *continues to read.*

BEA. What?

SOPHIE. Isn't it? It must be. Jack?

JACK. What's going on?

SOPHIE. Oh, there you are! I was just saying that it must be the time that normally you come home from school.

BEA. We're on our school holidays.

SOPHIE. Yes, I know, but –

JACK. What time is it?

SOPHIE. Why, around five, I think, there's no clock in this… I'd have to check to be exact.

JACK. Yes, you would. But if that's the time, to answer your question, normally we'd be back earlier.

BEA. We're back in time for tea normally.

JACK. Is it teatime?

SOPHIE. It can be if you want it to be.

   ...

   Well?

JACK. I've never wanted it to be teatime before. It just was teatime.

BEA. I want it to be teatime at lunchtime sometimes.

JACK. At school.

BEA. Yeah, when all you've got is double Geography –

JACK. Yes, then you want it to be teatime.

SOPHIE. But you don't want it to be teatime now?

JACK. We've never been at teatime and it's not teatime. It just is, when it is.

SOPHIE. Right… And it isn't now?

BEA. It can't be.

SOPHIE. Why not?

BEA. I don't know.

JACK. It's one of those things.

BEA. You can't create a sunset, for example.

...

That might sound a funny thing to say –

JACK. I understand it.

SOPHIE. I don't.

JACK. You wouldn't.

BEA. I bet Sophie makes her own tea.

SOPHIE. Of course I do.

JACK. It's just there for us.

BEA. It's part of the day.

JACK. Yes.

Not any more.

SOPHIE. Let me take care of it.

JACK. It's not the same.

SOPHIE. Well, of course it isn't, but –

JACK. No…

SOPHIE. Jack?

...

BEA. What's wrong with you, you idiot?

JACK. Oh, we're being stupid.

BEA. I'm not, you might be – you can be stupid if you want –

JACK. We've got to –

BEA. Suits me fine, you stupid idiot –

JACK. No, Bea, we've got to –

BEA. I'll be the big-brain brainbox –

JACK. No, listen, we've got to make the days now.

BEA. What, like Lego?

JACK. Yes, like Lego. But we've missed it today. Tomorrow, we'll be ready ready ready.

BEA. Ready ready ready like rabbits rabbits rabbits.

JACK. What?

BEA. You know…

JACK. Don't be an idiot.

BEA finds this increasingly funny.

BEA. Sorry…

SOPHIE. Perhaps we'll have some dinner later on, instead?

JACK. If you want, Sophie.

BEA. She does – she's probably starving –

SOPHIE. Well, I can wait, although my tummy is rumbling a little bit.

BEA. Rumbling ready ready ready rabbits rabbits rabbits running in the warren warren warren –

JACK. Rumble-Bumble-Bea –

BEA. Bumble-Rumble-Bea…

…

JACK. Bumble-Bea was bitter,
    Bumble-Bea was sour,
    Bumble-Bea got better
    From the Bumble-Honey Flower.

This rhyme strikes a chord with SOPHIE.

BEA. I am the Bumble-Bea!

BEA 'flies' around the room, perhaps repeating the phrase, making flying noises.

When she stops, she picks up her book. Then so does JACK.

…

SOPHIE. Jack – ?

JACK. What?

SOPHIE. It's nothing really, I –

JACK. What?

SOPHIE. That little poem you just –

JACK. What about it?

SOPHIE. Just that I think I remember your father saying it to you both when you were little.

JACK. He could've said it, but I invented it.

SOPHIE. Really? You were very young –

JACK. Dad told me that I invented it.

BEA. I remember Jack making it up.

JACK. So do I.

...

SOPHIE. Maybe I'm mistaken.

SOPHIE *exits*.

Scene Five

Later the same day. Early evening.

JACK *and* BEA *are still dressed and are reading as before. More books are strewn about and piled up.*

SOPHIE *enters*.

...

SOPHIE. Well then. Good evening to you both.

JACK. What's happened?

SOPHIE. Oh, nothing, nothing's happened at all. Just saying good evening.

JACK. You look happy.

BEA. You do, you've got a nice smile. Dad says you're a happy sort of person.

JACK. Like Mum.

SOPHIE. Did he? Well, I like to think that I'm a happy sort of person. I like to look on the bright side of things if I can.

JACK. That's definitely a good thing to do. Mum says that a lot.

BEA. 'Look on the bright side, for the bright side's always brighter.'

SOPHIE. Yes. Yes, she did say that, didn't she.

JACK. It doesn't make much sense to me, but I think it is a nice sentiment.

BEA. Jack, you're such a brainbox.

SOPHIE. Well, it makes sense to me.

BEA. It makes sense to me too.

JACK. Suit yourselves.

JACK *returns to his book.*

...

SOPHIE. Well, I have an idea. How about we treat ourselves? We could order a takeaway and watch the telly together –

BEA. We can't do that.

SOPHIE. Why not?

JACK. We don't watch TV in the summer, because –

BEA. It's better to do outdoor things.

JACK. It's a rule.

SOPHIE. When do you start watching TV again?

JACK. After the holidays.

BEA. When we go back to school.

JACK. We're not allowed. Anyway, we could try to watch it, but it wouldn't work.

SOPHIE. Why not?

JACK. Dad's taken the fuse out.

SOPHIE. Oh.

JACK. He does it every summer since we were little.

BEA. Oh, it used to drive me bonkers, 'cos you'd try to watch it, but when you tried to turn it on, it just wouldn't work and I never knowed why!

JACK. Dad does this trick –

BEA. Yeah, it's like magic, isn't it?

JACK. But it's not really.

BEA. Yeah, it's not really, obviously. He brings us in here and says –

JACK. 'Let's watch TV together.'

BEA. Or –

JACK. 'There's a really good film on – '

BEA. Or something. Then he says –

JACK. 'Now you two go and brush your teeth – '

BEA. Or something else like –

JACK. 'Go and get us a packet of crisps each.'

BEA. And we go out of the room and do what he wants us to do –

JACK. And then we come back in –

BEA. And he says –

JACK. 'Go on, turn it on then, you little scamps.'

BEA. And then we turn it on, but it doesn't come on and I just don't know why 'cos the telly always works, doesn't it? And then Dad says –

JACK. 'Oh no, what have you done? You've broken the telly!'

BEA. And we're all 'Aaarrgh!' 'cos we think we have, 'cos we look behind the telly and the plug is still in!

JACK. He's taken the fuse out, but I didn't know about fuses then.

BEA. We know now.

JACK. Obviously.

SOPHIE. Of course.

BEA. And then Dad says –

JACK. 'Well, you know what this means?'

BEA. And we say –

JACK *and* BEA. 'Oh no, what?'

BEA. And then… and then he says –

JACK. 'The summer has finally arrived. It's time – '

JACK *and* BEA. ' – for that telly to have a holiday, just like you.'

BEA. And he always does it on the first day of school holidays, but we always forget!

JACK. We always forgot.

BEA. He did it this year.

SOPHIE. Ingenious.

BEA. Mum likes us to read more books and do outdoor things.

SOPHIE. I couldn't agree more.

Well, we'll have to find some exciting things to do, won't we?

BEA. We go on holiday –

JACK. To the seaside.

SOPHIE. Let me have a think and I'll try and come up with some fun things to do over the next few days.

JACK. If you want.

BEA. Yeah.

JACK. We've only got two days till we go on holiday, you know.

SOPHIE. Jack, darling, I don't think that this year –

JACK. We always go on holiday the day after our birthday.

SOPHIE. It's your birthday the day after tomorrow? Oh God, it had completely slipped my mind –

BEA. Don't worry, I hadn't forgotten about it.

SOPHIE. I'm sure you haven't –

JACK. We leave really early the next morning –

BEA. Yeah, it's Mum's idea – it's really clever 'cos we sleep all the way there 'cos we're so tired from our birthday party.

JACK. My mum's always got a trick up her sleeve.

BEA. We've done it since we were little. Did you come with us on holiday?

SOPHIE. When?

BEA. After the shouting birthday?

SOPHIE. No, no, I didn't.

BEA. I bet we were really tired after that birthday.

SOPHIE. Right, well, I'm sure we can find a way to celebrate your birthday properly here, even if we can't go to the seaside like you normally –

JACK. Yes, we can.

...

SOPHIE. Jack? What's the matter?

BEA. Jack?

...

SOPHIE. Jack –

JACK. Why did you say that?

SOPHIE. Say what, darling?

JACK. I'm still going on my holidays – we're still going on our –

SOPHIE. Jack, I'm sorry, but I can't take you on –

JACK. Why not?

SOPHIE. Jack, I know how much you might want to, but I... –

JACK. Why not?

SOPHIE. I don't have much – enough money... –

JACK. Why?

SOPHIE. And there's no car – I'm sorry, look, I didn't mean to say that – I mean, I don't own a car, I can't even drive, so –

JACK. I'm going on holiday with Mum and Dad.

SOPHIE. What?

JACK. Isn't that right, BeaBea?

BEA. Yeah.

SOPHIE. Children –

JACK. Don't call us that.

SOPHIE. Jack –

BEA. Don't fight, don't fight –

JACK. You're not our mum.

SOPHIE. Jack, that is most unfair.

BEA. He didn't mean it, Sophie. Did you, Jack?

JACK. Why are you taking her side?

BEA. I'm not, I'm not, I just don't want you to fight – I know she's not my mum – why did you say that? – even I know that, stupid.

JACK. That's not what I said –

SOPHIE. Please –

JACK. She's saying we're not going on holiday and we are – she's talking to us like she's Mum.

BEA. No, I don't think so – I don't think Sophie's like my mum at all –

JACK. But that's it! By saying things like Mum, she's saying we're not going on holiday any more and we are, we are! Because it's the time, and the day it is – then we know, don't we? We know – we know what to do.

BEA. I know what to do, don't I?

JACK. Of course you do. We know together.

SOPHIE. I think it's time for bed, don't you?

JACK. What time is it? I want to know what time it is.

SOPHIE. Bedtime.

JACK. Bea, do you know what time it is?

BEA. I want to go to bed now.

JACK. It must be time then. Goodnight, Sophie. Sorry for getting shouty.

BEA. I'm sorry too.

SOPHIE. Sleep well.

JACK *and* BEA. Goodnight.

> JACK *and* BEA *exit.*

Scene Six

Middle of the night. Darkness.

SOPHIE *is asleep on the sofa, fully clothed.*

The room is as before.

JACK *enters, still in his suit. He stands in the doorway, momentarily. He takes a few steps into the room and then sees the figure lying on the sofa. He stares.*

JACK. Mum…

> SOPHIE *stirs a little.*

> Mum, I'm scared.

SOPHIE *drowsily awakes, still half-dreaming.*

SOPHIE. Philip...

JACK. Mum?

SOPHIE. Philip...

JACK. Yes.

...

JACK *turns on the lamp, the light shining towards* SOPHIE.

SOPHIE. What? Christ... who is that? Jack?

JACK. Hello.

SOPHIE. What time is it?

JACK. I don't know.

Bedtime.

SOPHIE. God, look at me. Sorry.

JACK. Don't worry, I slept in my clothes too. See?

SOPHIE. So you did.

Tramps together.

JACK. I wouldn't mind being a tramp.

SOPHIE. It's better to have a roof over your head, darling.

JACK. Yes.

SOPHIE. Are you alright?

JACK. I'm fine, thanks. I fell asleep on Mum and Dad's bed. I was having a nightmare.

SOPHIE. Oh, Jack, are you upset?

JACK. I said I was fine, Sophie, thank you. It's over now.

SOPHIE. Are you sure? Do you want to –

JACK. I woke up really quickly and then I was wide awake and I couldn't get back to sleep. I didn't want to particularly. When you think about how long I've been sleeping, then you might say that I've had quite enough sleep already.

SOPHIE. You could indeed say that.

JACK. I'm not sure if I'll try to get back to sleep. I might just stay up and read.

SOPHIE. I think maybe you should go back to bed –

JACK. Mum would say I have to go back to sleep, as it's still night, and we've got a long day tomorrow.

SOPHIE. Have you?

JACK. What?

SOPHIE. Got a long day tomorrow. You two little conspirators haven't told me if you've made any plans.

JACK. What's a conspirator?

SOPHIE. Oh, it doesn't matter, I was only joking.

JACK. No, tell me, I'd like to know.

SOPHIE. Bea and you are always talking away together and making little plans…

JACK. I suppose we do.

SOPHIE. I'm not saying that's bad –

JACK. Why would it be? Is conspirator a bad thing?

SOPHIE. Not necessarily.

JACK. So it's like making a plan.

SOPHIE. A secret plan, maybe.

JACK. I haven't, you know. I haven't been making a secret plan.

SOPHIE. I'm glad. But that doesn't mean you can't – I mean, if I had a brother I'm sure I'd be making secret plans all the time.

JACK. Don't you have a brother or a sister?

SOPHIE. No, I don't.

JACK. Are you an only child?

SOPHIE. Yes, I am.

JACK. Are you an orphan?

SOPHIE. Well, my mum and dad are dead.

JACK. I'm an orphan now.

SOPHIE. Yes, but I'm here to look after you.

JACK. Yes.

...

You called me Philip.

SOPHIE. What?

JACK. Just now. Before the light was on.

SOPHIE. Did I – ?

JACK. Were you dreaming of Dad?

SOPHIE. Well... maybe I was, I'm not sure...

JACK. So was I.

SOPHIE. I'm sure you were.

JACK. Why are you sure? I don't always dream about them, you know. I'm not obsessed or anything.

It's funny... funny that you called me Philip...

SOPHIE. I didn't mean to frighten you, I was probably still dreaming –

JACK. You didn't frighten me, so don't worry. I meant it's funny because I called you Mum.

SOPHIE. Did you?

JACK. Yes, I called you Mum. I didn't call you her name – I didn't call you Ros, like you called me Philip – I just called you Mum. Didn't you hear me?

SOPHIE. No, no, I didn't –

JACK. I called you Mum when I came in the room and the light was still off and you were lying on the sofa.

SOPHIE. Did you... did you think you saw Ros? I mean, your mum?

JACK. No, of course not, she's dead.

SOPHIE. Of course, Jack. That doesn't mean you didn't see her, or thought she might be here.

JACK. Don't be silly, I'm not an idiot: she's dead, dead as a doornail, dead as a dodo. Done for. Ashes to ashes and dust to dust.

SOPHIE. Fine.

JACK. I think maybe I was still sleeping too. Sleepwalking. That would be a rational explanation for that exchange.

SOPHIE. Do you think you were sleepwalking?

JACK. How would I know? If I did know, then I wouldn't have been sleepwalking, would I? Maybe I was just daydreaming. Either way, there isn't any way we can find out now, as that moment has passed and we can't turn back the clock.

SOPHIE. No, we can't, you're right. You were probably sleepwalking.

JACK. That seems the most likely explanation.

Do you think, if I turned off the light, it might happen again?

SOPHIE. No, I don't think so. I'm wide awake now.

JACK *turns off the lamp. Darkness.*

Jack, come on – turn the light back on.

JACK. Mum.

SOPHIE. Jack, that's not funny.

JACK. Mum, I'm scared... –

SOPHIE. Stop it, Jack – turn the light back on.

...

You can't just go about getting your own way all the time.

SOPHIE *turns on the lamp.* JACK*'s hand is still holding the switch-string as she does so. As the light comes on, he holds her hand.*

JACK. 'Forgive me.'

SOPHIE. Jack, it's fine, just please, in future, try to listen –

JACK. 'Forget me.'

SOPHIE. What?

JACK. 'Forget me.'

SOPHIE. Jack, you're not making any sense –

JACK. But you said it before.

SOPHIE. What? When? No, I didn't –

JACK. You did –

SOPHIE. I did not, Jack –

JACK. Sorry, Sophie, don't get angry, I was just trying an experiment.

SOPHIE. Look, sometimes when someone asks you politely not to do something, the polite response is not to do it.

JACK. But it might have worked.

SOPHIE. What might have? Jack, it is very late and I'm sorry, but you are being quite exasperating.

JACK. You did look a little like Mum though. When the light was off. You couldn't really see her face.

SOPHIE. Really. Well, that's very interesting, sweetheart.

JACK. Did I look like Dad?

SOPHIE. What? Jack, the light was off. Perhaps you should go back to bed, darling.

JACK. Maybe it's time travel when I turned off the light.

SOPHIE. What on earth do you mean? Please, Jack, come on –

JACK. Did I look like Dad in the dark?

SOPHIE. Jack, I couldn't see you properly –

JACK. Yes, as it was dark, but in the dark, did I? Please, please just say.

SOPHIE. Jack, I didn't think about it, it didn't cross my mind. Now stop this.

JACK. Please, you must know.

SOPHIE. Well, you are almost as tall as him.

JACK. So I almost fooled you, didn't I?

SOPHIE. No.

No.

JACK. It doesn't matter. As an experiment it was flawed, but definitely of interest. We'll find other ways to explore it.

SOPHIE *takes his hand.*

SOPHIE. Jack, please, go back to bed.

I'm going to go to bed too.

...

BEA *appears in the doorway in her black dress, looking very sleepy, but also distressed. She has clearly been sleeping fully clothed too.*

JACK *sees her and immediately turns the light back off.*

SOPHIE *does not see her.*

BEA *freezes to the spot.*

JACK. Mummy.

SOPHIE *and* BEA *speak the next two lines simultaneously.*

SOPHIE. What?

BEA. Daddy?

SOPHIE (*hears* BEA, *which makes her jump*). Oh God!

BEA *lets out a shocked, involuntary shout of terror at this sudden noise.*

JACK. Bea!

JACK *turns the light back on.* BEA *is frightened, on the edge of panic.*

BEA. Jack!

JACK. Bea –

BEA. Jack! Jack!

SOPHIE. Bea, it's okay –

JACK. Leave her alone! Quiet, Bea, shhhh –

BEA. I had a dream –

JACK. Me too, me too –

BEA. Daddy and Mummy were shouting at me –

JACK. No, they never did, BeaBea –

BEA. But I couldn't stop them, then I woke up and I heard them downstairs –

JACK. No, no, you didn't –

BEA. But I walked down the stairs and Mummy was angry at Daddy and then it was very quiet and I thought they'd gone away again –

JACK. No, they haven't, they haven't gone away –

BEA. But it went dark and I thought Mummy was shouting at me –

JACK. No, BeaBea, Sophie was shouting at me –

BEA. Why?

JACK. Because –

BEA. Why did it go dark again?

JACK. Because… I was playing a joke.

BEA. I never want it to go dark again.

JACK. Sorry.

BEA. Can we go on our holiday now?

JACK. Not yet, BeaBea, we can't go yet.

    JACK *holds her.*

    Sorry Bumble-Bea.

BEA. Why isn't it bedtime?

JACK. It is bedtime definitely now. Definitely.

...

SOPHIE. You two go on up to bed.

Jack?

JACK. Yes?

SOPHIE. We'll talk about this in the morning.

BEA. Talk about what?

JACK. Oh, the joke I was playing.

BEA. What joke?

JACK. Don't worry, it was nothing, it was like an experiment. I'll tell you about it in bed.

BEA. But I'm not sleepy now.

JACK. No, I'm not either, but remember what Mum says?

SOPHIE. It's still night-time and you've got a long day tomorrow.

BEA. I miss Mummy.

JACK. We've got a long day tomorrow. Know why?

BEA. Why?

JACK. 'Cos it's still the summer and the sun is up for longer.

BEA. I'm going to be up with the lark.

JACK. Sophie?

SOPHIE. What?

JACK. We'll see you when the sun rises and the cock is crowing.

BEA. Night, Sophie. Sorry for being such a crybaby.

SOPHIE. Don't you worry, little Bea, I quite understand.

BEA. I miss my mum.

SOPHIE. I know, darling, I know.

JACK. Let's go to bed.

> JACK *and* BEA *exit, hand in hand.*

> SOPHIE *sits on the sofa. She switches off the lamp.*

Scene Seven

A few hours later. The half-light just before dawn.

SOPHIE *is asleep on the couch.*

The room is as before.

BEA *enters, standing in the doorway. She is wearing a floral dress that is too big for her. She stays standing in the doorway a minute.*

The first rays of sunrise shine weakly into the room through the French windows. BEA *moves into the light, facing the sun. She stands still a moment, then she quietly begins to dance: pirouetting gently on the spot. She's a clumsy dancer; her moves reflect a year's worth of basic ballet classes.*

SOPHIE *wakes up slowly. She watches* BEA.

BEA *notices* SOPHIE *is awake. She waves at her. She continues to dance.*

BEA. Morning, Sophie.

> BEA *concludes her dance with a final clumsy pirouette.*

> I'm not very good, am I?

> I'm getting better though.

> *She looks out into the sunlight.*

> ...

SOPHIE. That's a very beautiful dress you're wearing.

BEA. I've never worn it before.

SOPHIE. Where did you find it?

BEA. In Mum's wardrobe. She wears it a lot. It's a bit big for me. But I like it. I could get fat in it and you'd never know.

I do my dancing practice before breakfast because Jack thinks I'm a clodhopper. He can't see me now.

SOPHIE. I don't think you're a clodhopper.

BEA. Well, I am a big old clodhopper. I don't mind.

SOPHIE. I think your dancing's very / beautiful.

BEA. Clod. Hopper.

SOPHIE. Well, actually –

BEA. I'm a hodclopper.

...

SOPHIE. If you insist.

BEA. Do you dance, Sophie?

SOPHIE. No no no.

BEA. Why not?

SOPHIE. Oh, I don't know... I think I just get embarrassed.

BEA. Why? Don't you think it's fun?

SOPHIE. No. No, I don't.

BEA. Why, because you're an embarrassment?

SOPHIE. That's right – what?

BEA. Why don't you do it by yourself like me?

SOPHIE. Well, I... I don't really have the space.

BEA. Don't be silly, don't you have a living room?

SOPHIE. Yes, but it's... it's very small.

BEA. Oh.

Is your house very small?

SOPHIE. I don't have a beautiful house like this, unfortunately. I have a... a little flat.

BEA. I think you could be a dancer if you wanted.

SOPHIE. I think you might be wrong about that.

BEA. You move quite gracefully, but you have rather bad posture.

SOPHIE. Oh.

BEA. That's not my opinion. It's what my teacher would say.

SOPHIE. Well, maybe you can show me how to do it one day.

BEA. 'Hold your head up high.'

SOPHIE. It's a little early, Bea.

BEA. No, not now, silly, that's what she says to me because I'm always looking at my toes.

Mum always says it too: 'Hold your head up high. Life will knock you, but hold your head up high.'

I find that difficult because I'm always looking at my toes.

SOPHIE. Are you always up this early?

BEA. I'm a restless little girl.

SOPHIE. It's been quite a night.

BEA. Sorry for waking you up.

SOPHIE. Oh, you didn't wake me up. You were quiet as a mouse.

BEA. I just wanted to do my dancing. I have to do my dancing.

SOPHIE. Have you been awake since you last went upstairs?

BEA. What happened before with Jack?

SOPHIE. I think he had a nasty nightmare.

BEA. He gets them a lot. I have to look after him.

SOPHIE. It seems to me that you two look after each other.

BEA. He needs looking after. I know it. I've got to keep my beady eyes on him.

SOPHIE. You're both in very capable hands.

BEA. You're like a guardian angel.

SOPHIE. No, I'm not.

BEA. I believe in you, like a guardian angel.

SOPHIE. Thank you, that's very flattering.

BEA. For me it's just a realistic thing to say. I trust you to keep your beady eyes on us, especially Jack.

SOPHIE. I'll keep my eyes on both of you, don't you worry.

BEA. But especially Jack, because he's a boy and he's a troublemaker.

SOPHIE. Do you think so?

BEA. Oh, Sophie, you're ever so polite, aren't you?

SOPHIE. Whatever do you mean?

BEA. I know you have to love him lots because you're his godmum, but even I know that all girls think that little boys are horrid.

SOPHIE. I was once told boys are beastly but girls are ghastly.

BEA. Who told you that?

SOPHIE. Your mother used to say it when the pair of you were very little.

BEA. Really?

SOPHIE. Yes.

BEA. She's never said that to me.

SOPHIE. Well, she did, but perhaps you were a little too small to understand.

BEA. I hate that. I hate it. I wish I could remember everything.

SOPHIE. Well, now you know she said it.

BEA. I'll pretend I remembered it.

SOPHIE. But I'll know I told you.

BEA. Can't it be our secret, Sophie?

SOPHIE. Of course, darling, it's only a little lie.

BEA. Don't call it a lie.

SOPHIE. Bea, it doesn't matter.

BEA. No, no, don't call it a lie. It's a memory, isn't it?
Memories aren't lies, are they? Just because I was a baby
doesn't mean I can't remember it now you've reminded me.
You just need to have a remember and a reminder, then it all
comes back to you with a whoosh.

SOPHIE. You think you can remember now?

BEA. Yes.

What's wrong with that?

SOPHIE. Nothing, darling. Let's not say any more about it.

BEA. Sometimes you've never remembered things and then
you do, all of a sudden. How am I to know what's still to be
remembered? When you came to pick us up I remembered
instantly when we had our birthday party and Mum and Dad
shouted. And I'd never thought of that before. I didn't even
know it had happened. But it did.

SOPHIE. How funny.

BEA. Don't you remember it?

SOPHIE. Not very well, it's a long time ago now.

BEA. We all had our party hats on, didn't we?

SOPHIE. Yes, I think we did.

BEA. And Mum got shouty outside with Dad and, oh yeah – then
a door slammed shut or something and then we went to bed.

SOPHIE. You may well be right.

BEA. It can happen, see?

BEA *turns back to the sun.*

She turns back round.

Will you do dancing with me, Sophie?

SOPHIE. No, I couldn't possibly.

BEA. 'No, I couldn't possibly.' Oh, come on.

SOPHIE. Bea, really, *really*, absolutely not, I'm an awful, awful dancer.

BEA. I don't care. I'm a clodhopper, so you'll only be as bad as me.

SOPHIE. No, really, I can't.

BEA. Come on, come on, come on.

SOPHIE. Bea...

...

BEA. Sometimes I wake up this early and come down and I see Mum standing right here, looking out at the sun rising on the garden. She wears this dress sometimes when I've seen her. I'm in my jim-jams though.

She stands here all quiet just looking out of the window and I know she's just like me because she obviously woke up straight away very early too, just like me. I stand still and look at her sometimes. Mostly I say hello and she gives me a kiss and walks into the kitchen and puts the kettle on. Then I do my dancing practice.

Dad and Jack are fast asleep and they never saw it. Not once. But Mum comes back in with her tea and watches me here. In this spot, right here, watching me be a right old clodhopper. Then once she finishes her tea she comes over and helps me a bit. And we dance together a bit. Then she gives me a kiss and goes to wake up Dad.

So, come on. Come on, Sophie. Then I'll go and wake up Jack.

SOPHIE. What do you want me to do?

BEA. Just hold my hands as I practise pirouetting on my tip-toes.

SOPHIE *does this*.

SOPHIE. How am I doing?

BEA. Carry on.

BEA *is looking at her toes*.

SOPHIE. Hold your head up high.

BEA. Aaarrgh! I know, I know!

They continue.

They stop.

...

Well done you.

SOPHIE. Thank you.

BEA. What time is it?

SOPHIE. It's still very early, darling.

BEA. Are you going to be here for ever?

SOPHIE. I...

BEA. Do you want to be?

SOPHIE. I have to be.

BEA. We have to fill the gaps.

...

SOPHIE. What do you mean?

BEA. Like a jigsaw.

SOPHIE. Bea, what do you mean by that?

BEA. Jack and me were talking about it.

SOPHIE. About what?

BEA. Is that what the phrase 'picking up the pieces' means?

SOPHIE. 'Picking up the pieces'?

BEA. We read it in some book. It said something like: 'When something as terrible as this happens, only the children are left to pick up the pieces.' Something like that. And I thought, what pieces do I have to pick up? And I've been looking around and I think it's like a jigsaw puzzle, where you have to pick up all the pieces to complete the picture all over again. And we just got to figure out what those pieces are. It's like a quiz. Like a game of hide-and-seek or something. I'm going to have a morning bath now.

BEA *moves to go.*

SOPHIE. Bea –

BEA. Put the kettle on. Mum puts the kettle on.

SOPHIE. Bea –

But she's left the room.

SOPHIE *is left alone.*

Bright sunlight pours into the room.

Scene Eight

A couple of hours later. It is still early.

SOPHIE *is sitting, still looking dishevelled.*

The room is as before.

She gets up and goes towards the door to the rest of the house. A picture on the wall behind the door catches her eye, making her stop in her tracks. It is of a youthful Philip and Ros, JACK and BEA's parents. She stares at it. She touches it. She chokes back tears.

The door opens and JACK and BEA enter quietly, holding hands. The door hides SOPHIE momentarily. She uses this moment to gather herself.

BEA *is still dressed in her mother's floral dress, which remains too big for her.* JACK *is now wearing some of his father's clothes, which are also slightly too big for him. His smart shirt is baggy and his hands only peek out of the sleeves. His smart trousers have been folded up at the bottom so he doesn't trip up. He even wears a tie, done up rather neatly. His shoes are his own, and smart.*

SOPHIE *steps out from behind the door.*

SOPHIE. Good morning.

This shocks BEA *and* JACK. BEA *shrieks.* JACK *jumps, but remains silent.*

I'm sorry, I didn't mean to shock you.

JACK. Where did you come from?

SOPHIE. I was just... just standing by the door when you opened it.

JACK. Well, that makes sense.

BEA. You gave me the heebee-jeebies.

SOPHIE. I'm sorry, I really didn't mean to.

SOPHIE *takes in what* JACK *is wearing.*

You look very smart, Jack.

JACK. You look like you've been dragged through a hedge backwards.

SOPHIE. Jack.

Well, I slept on the sofa, remember?

JACK. I didn't mean to be rude.

SOPHIE. Well, you managed quite effortlessly.

BEA. Jack, say sorry to Sophie.

It's not her fault that she fell asleep on the sofa, or that you came in being a scaredy-cat in the middle of the night.

JACK. I had a nightmare.

BEA. That's not Sophie's fault, is it?

SOPHIE. Bea, thank you, but I can defend myself.

BEA. Say sorry.

JACK. Sorry, Sophie.

SOPHIE. Nevermind.

BEA. And I'm sorry I took so long having a bath. I just couldn't get out. I was daydreaming and daydreaming for ages.

JACK. I'm not in a bad mood. What I mean is, you still look very sleepy.

SOPHIE. I didn't get a huge amount of sleep.

JACK. Why didn't you come upstairs to bed?

SOPHIE. I don't know, Jack. I just fell asleep. I must have been very tired. I don't remember, I just fell asleep.

JACK. Have you been crying?

SOPHIE. Who me? No…

JACK. Your eyes are all red.

SOPHIE. Like I said, I haven't had much sleep.

BEA. You're going to sleep like a log tonight.

…

JACK walks up to SOPHIE.

JACK. Sorry, Sophie.

He kisses her on the cheek.

SOPHIE *is taken aback.*

He then walks back and holds BEA*'s hand. He swings it.*

You're very pretty, you know.

SOPHIE. What?

JACK. What do you think, darling?

BEA. Very pretty indeed, darling, but her posture could be better.

JACK. Yes, I think you're right.

SOPHIE. You two are quite…

JACK. I'm just saying, that's all. I would have said it before, but it didn't seem quite right. There's a time and a place for everything.

SOPHIE. How very romantic of you.

JACK. I don't mean it to be romantic. It's a fact, I think. I'm not making it up.

BEA. Dad says you're very pretty.

SOPHIE. Really? Does – did he? He liked to tease me. A lot.

JACK. I remembered. Dad always said he's the sort of man that calls a spade a spade. So do I, I think.

SOPHIE. You're certainly very direct and to the point.

JACK. Some people think I'm rude, don't they, Bea?

BEA. Yeah – it's so boring, last term I had to stop the big boys flushing his head down the loo –

JACK. Sophie –

BEA. I'm his guardian angel –

JACK. Why don't you have a husband and some children?

SOPHIE. Jack.

JACK. That was direct and to the point, wasn't it?

BEA. Very much so, darling.

JACK. Thank you, darling.

BEA. That's a spade's a spade.

SOPHIE. Jack, that is an extremely rude question to ask. Sometimes people like to keep an element of their private lives entirely private.

BEA. You're such a nosy parker.

JACK. Yes, that was a rude question. I didn't think it would be, but it was.

SOPHIE. Yes, it was, and you shouldn't ask such questions, do you understand?

...

JACK *walks up to* SOPHIE.

JACK. Sorry, Sophie.

He kisses her on the cheek.

He then walks back and holds BEA*'s hand. He swings it again.*

SOPHIE *has to turn away.*

BEA *swings round and drags* JACK *over to the garden door, where the sun shines in.* BEA *opens the door and they go outside.*

SOPHIE *struggles with herself. No noise comes from the garden.*

SOPHIE *notices she can't hear* JACK *and* BEA. *She walks over to the windows to see where they are. She takes a shocked step back.*

...

SOPHIE. Jack! Beatrice! Come here! This instant!

Right now!

JACK *and* BEA *re-enter. They stand just inside the doorway, holding hands.*

...

Well?

BEA. We were just playing.

SOPHIE. Playing?

JACK. What's wrong, Sophie?

SOPHIE. Please don't try my patience, Jack.

JACK. I'm not trying to try your patience, Sophie.

SOPHIE. Yes, you are, Jack.

BEA. Please don't get angry, we were just playing a game.

SOPHIE. You must never, never do that.

BEA. Do what?

SOPHIE. Beatrice, please don't play innocent with me, you know very well what I mean, and you must *never* do that *ever* again.

JACK. Sophie, I think I understand why you're so upset.

SOPHIE. Oh, you do? Well, I'm glad. Perhaps you could inform your sister.

JACK. Certainly.

Bea, she's angry because we were kissing each other.

BEA. Oh.

JACK. Am I right, Sophie?

SOPHIE. Yes, Jack, that is exactly right.

BEA. But it was just a game.

SOPHIE. You must never play games like that!

BEA *is upset.*

JACK. Look what you've done.

SOPHIE. How dare you say that to me.

JACK. You can't speak to me! You're not allowed!

JACK *runs out into the garden.*

BEA. No...

...

It's just a game we're playing, that's all.

SOPHIE. You must never, ever play games like that – how, how is that a game?

Beatrice, you'll have to explain to me how kissing your brother is an acceptable game to be playing.

BEA. We've got to make our own days now – we've got to pick up the pieces, don't we? Aren't you picking up the pieces? Jack says you don't have a mum and dad either.

SOPHIE. What? I... I... I can't see how my parents have any-thing to do with this.

BEA. Don't you feel like your mummy is part of you?

SOPHIE. My mother is dead, Bea.

BEA. My mummy... my mummy is a part of me and... and all we've got to do is pick up the pieces.

SOPHIE. I don't understand –

BEA. Oh, Jack always says it so much better!

SOPHIE. What does Jack say?

BEA. I thought you'd understand.

SOPHIE. What does Jack say, Bea?

BEA. Don't you know how to do it? I thought… I thought you could show us.

BEA *runs out into the garden.*

SOPHIE. Bea!

SOPHIE *doesn't give chase.*

Scene Nine

Two hours later.

SOPHIE *is on the telephone to the police.*

SOPHIE. Well, I'm very sorry, but I think there is something to worry about – I'm not trying to tell you how to do your job, but we're in the absolute middle of nowhere, they could be miles away by now, I mean, they could be lost in the middle of that enormous forest… Well, of course they may come back at any moment, but it's been two hours since we, since we, well, had this row… Yes, exactly, I'm worried for their safety…

BEA *runs into the room through the windows and straight out through the door to the rest of the house.*

BEA. Sorry, Sophie!

SOPHIE. Oh Jesus! Bea!… Yes, that was one of them – Bea! – I'm sorry, I'm going to have to go.

SOPHIE *puts the phone down.*

JACK *appears in the garden doorway, unbeknownst to* SOPHIE, *who is following* BEA.

Bea!

JACK. Hello there.

SOPHIE *jumps in shock.*

SOPHIE. Oh Christ!

JACK. Sorry, I didn't mean to frighten you.

SOPHIE. Jack.

JACK. Got you back.

SOPHIE. Yes. Yes, you did.

JACK. I didn't do it on purpose, Sophie. I didn't frighten you
on purpose.

...

SOPHIE. Well, neither did I earlier.

JACK. You frightened Bea earlier.

SOPHIE. I know, but I was very angry. At what I saw the pair
of you –

JACK. No, not that, when you came out from behind the door
like a jack-in-the-box.

She screamed like a ghost. Like a girl.

SOPHIE. Jack, would you like to sit down?

JACK. Why?

SOPHIE. So we can have a talk.

JACK. When you shouted earlier, that upset Bea, but I don't
think it frightened her. She's been shouted at before. Both of
us have.

SOPHIE. Yes, well, I regret shouting at her, but I was very upset
by what I saw.

And that's what I'd like to talk about, so would you like to
sit down?

JACK. No thank you.

SOPHIE. Jack, please, don't be difficult, I just want to talk to
you, that's all.

JACK. So do I.

SOPHIE. You do?

JACK. Yes.

I don't want to sit down though.

SOPHIE. Alright. Fine.

JACK. What do you think of my clothes?

SOPHIE. I'm certainly glad you're not wearing that black suit any more.

JACK. Do you think they suit me? Do I look like I'm top-of-the-tree?

SOPHIE. You look very smart. You both do. Where's Bea? Has she gone out again?

JACK. No, she's gone upstairs. I'm here to have a talk with you. We were in the woods, us two together, being conspirators.

SOPHIE. What were you doing in the woods?

JACK. Didn't you want to come and find us?

SOPHIE. Yes, yes, I did want to come and find you, Jack, but I don't know my way around here, and I didn't think you'd be gone for so bloody long.

JACK. Well, we bloody well were, weren't we?

SOPHIE. I beg your pardon?

JACK. Gone a long time. We bloody well were gone a bloody long time.

SOPHIE. Jack, you shouldn't swear like that.

JACK. I over-egged that pudding, didn't I?

SOPHIE. Yes, you did.

JACK. If Mum and Dad go for one of their long walks in the woods I get worried, even though they tell us where they've gone. I get a panic in my belly that builds up until it's like a fire and I almost can't bear it any longer. Didn't you feel that?

SOPHIE. I was very worried.

JACK. Sometimes we run and find them if they've been gone too long. Didn't you want to run and find us?

SOPHIE. Yes, I did, but I would have got lost, because I don't know the woods.

JACK. Are you scared?

SOPHIE. Scared? Scared of what?

JACK. Of going in the woods. Don't you play in the woods?

SOPHIE. I don't have a wood to play in, Jack.

JACK. Why not?

SOPHIE. Because... Because I live in a big city, I don't live near a wood, any sort of wood.

JACK. Didn't you ever walk in them with Mum and Dad?

SOPHIE. Sometimes, but it was a long time ago.

JACK. I know them really well. Mum, Bea and me build things in them, like traps and hiding places and stuff.

SOPHIE. Is that what you and Bea were doing just now?

JACK. When we run in to find them, when they've been gone a really long time, sometimes we find them just walking together and talking together and we find them because we can hear their voices through the trees. We sneak up on them and surprise them. Even though I have that panicky fire in my belly, I never call out their names to them. That's funny, isn't it? I don't know why I don't call out their names, because in my belly I think maybe they've gone away for ever. I think it's because I know they're in those woods somewhere. We always find them somehow.

SOPHIE. Jack.

JACK. What?

SOPHIE. Please don't be angry with me when I ask this, but do you still think that, maybe, that your mum and dad –

JACK. One time we went running to find them and we couldn't hear them talking at all and it felt like the fire was going to burst out of my mouth or something. And the moment that I was going to shout out 'Dad and Mum!' I thought I heard Mum singing. Or I thought it was singing. But then it stopped really quickly. It was confusing. Then I heard it again –

SOPHIE. Singing?

JACK. Like this:

(*Softly*.) 'Aaaaaahh.'

'Aaaaaahh.'

And we stopped dead still, because I knew it was Mum. For sure. And then she did it another time, but the note was a bit higher and by then I knew exactly where it was coming from. Then I think I heard Dad say Mum's name quite loudly. Then it was all quiet. And then Bea did the funniest thing: she sang it too.

'Aaaaaahh.'

I told her to shush, but Dad must have heard her because he shouted out our names and I was really annoyed for a moment, because I wanted to surprise them, and now we couldn't.

So we ran to where the singing came from, and we found them lying on the grass together beneath a big tree that Dad, Bea and me climb up sometimes. They were just lying on the grass, looking like they'd been running up a hill or something, all red faced and smiling. I asked them that: 'Have you been running up a hill or something?' But Dad just laughed, and I don't know why, but he just laughed. Not at me, just like it was really funny that I asked it. Oh, it's because obviously there aren't any hills close by. I admit it: it was a stupid thing to say. Mum got up and gave us both a kiss and we walked home for tea.

And that's what Bea and me were doing in the woods.

SOPHIE. What?

JACK. It's very simple really: after Bea ran out of the house, after she was crying, we ran off into the woods and lay by the tree. That's all. And Bea went 'Aaaaaahh.'

SOPHIE. That's all?

JACK. Yes.

SOPHIE. Jack, that's... that's...

JACK. Bea wanted me to come and tell you why we went to the woods and had a kiss on the lawn.

SOPHIE. And that's your answer?

JACK. Yes, I think it's very thorough.

SOPHIE. Jack, listen to me, I just want you to understand one simple thing.

JACK. What's that, Sophie?

SOPHIE. About you two kissing. When you were kissing each other.

JACK. Yes?

SOPHIE. You can't do that.

JACK. Why not?

SOPHIE. You just can't, Jack. It's not allowed to kiss your own sister. It's against the law.

JACK. But I wasn't.

SOPHIE. What? You just said you were. I saw you.

JACK. I wasn't.

SOPHIE. You were, Jack, you were. I'm sorry, but I'm in absolutely no mood for games.

JACK. We've got to make our own days up properly now and do the things that need to be done, don't we?

SOPHIE. I don't understand what you're talking about.

JACK. Weren't you listening to my story?

SOPHIE. Yes, yes, I was.

JACK. There are things we've got to do, Sophie.

SOPHIE. What things?

JACK. Well, at the start of the day, when it's early in the morning, we have to get up and get dressed for work. Even though it's holidays, I'm dressed for work today, because I think there will be things to do. I think that there will be work to do.

When I woke up this morning, when Bea was having a bath, I saw that it was a blue-sky day. When Bea came out of the bathroom she was wearing the summer dress, so then I remembered what we had to do for that morning moment when the summer sun is rising over the garden.

SOPHIE. What did you have to do?

JACK. These things just pop up. Like a jack-in-the-box. Like Bea says, you don't remember them till they happen.

If the sun is up bright and early and it's a blue-sky day, we walk out into the garden before I go to work. They stand in the sun and hold hands and they give each other a kiss. See? That way we can pick up the pieces and make the days again.

SOPHIE. Jack, do you think Mum and Dad are going to come back?

...

Jack? It's okay, darling, it's okay to tell me.

She approaches him.

Jack...

She holds his hands. JACK *looks down at them.*

Sweetheart, your mother and father –

JACK. Do you like these clothes?

...

SOPHIE. Jack.

JACK. Do I look smart?

SOPHIE. Smart?

Yes, you look very smart.

JACK. What do I look like?

He looks in her eyes. She can't hold his gaze and lets go of his hands.

He takes them back. She does not resist.

...

SOPHIE. Jack, I know you think this is some sort of game –

JACK. Who am I?

...

SOPHIE. Jack, this isn't funny.

JACK. Do you miss me?

SOPHIE. What?

He looks her right in the eyes.

JACK. Do you miss me?

SOPHIE *is distressed, but she doesn't move.*

SOPHIE. How can you say that to me?

...

JACK. I'm here.

SOPHIE. No...

JACK strokes SOPHIE's hair.

BEA enters and stands partially hidden at the doorway.

Neither JACK nor SOPHIE see her.

JACK kisses SOPHIE on the lips, lightly, and then lets go of SOPHIE's hands.

JACK sees BEA.

BEA exits. JACK follows.

Scene Ten

The next morning. Nine a.m.

It is raining lightly outside.

SOPHIE *is asleep on the sofa. She is dressed as before. She hasn't left the room.*

There is the sound of movement from other parts of the house. Then silence.

SOPHIE *wakes with a start. She doesn't move.*

More sounds from the house. This time, laughter can be heard. Then silence.

SOPHIE *moves to the windows. She looks out into the rain.*

The other door opens silently. JACK *and* BEA *enter tentatively, hand in hand. They are both carrying small suitcases.*

They are both dressed very smartly, as if for a party. BEA *is wearing an evening dress of her mother's. She has make-up on, but sloppily applied, reflecting her inexperience.* JACK *is in a smart suit of his father's, with a colourful shirt and tie. He has wet his hair and combed it over rather badly. Both wear their own shoes. Again, the clothes are too big for them.* JACK *has once again folded up the trousers and this time has rolled back the arms of the jacket.* BEA's *dress hangs off her, but she has pinned the bottom up, to avoid it dragging along the floor.*

JACK *and* BEA *put their suitcases down and step further into the room.* SOPHIE *hears this and turns around.*

JACK *and* BEA *are smiling, although they are trying not to, as if they can hardly stop themselves laughing.*

SOPHIE. Good morning.

   ...

BEA (*whispered*). Sophie?

SOPHIE. Yes?

BEA (*whispered*). What.

SOPHIE. What?

BEA. No no no, shush shush.

(*Whispered.*) What.

JACK (*whispered*). Day.

BEA (*whispered*). Is.

JACK (*whispered*). It.

BEA (*whispered*). Today?

SOPHIE. I...

BEA (*whispered*). What.

JACK (*whispered*). Day.

BEA (*whispered*). Is.

JACK (*whispered*). It.

BEA (*whispered*). Today?

SOPHIE. I, I don't know.

   ...

JACK. It's / Jack and Bea's birthday, stupid!

BEA. It's our birthday, stupid!

   JACK *and* BEA *run around the room in celebration.*

   They grab SOPHIE *and swing around several times. They let her go and twirl each other around until they are dizzy. They collapse, laughing.*

   Their laughter eventually dies once they have recovered their bearings.

SOPHIE. Happy birthday to the pair of you.

JACK. We're twins, but obviously we didn't come out of Mummy at the same time as each other. Bea came first.

BEA. Yeah, I'm older than Jack, I'm his big sister really.

JACK. Bea was crying all the time from the moment she popped out.

BEA. Like a jack-in-the-box –

JACK. But I didn't cry at all. I was quiet as a mouse when I was born.

BEA. We're exactly the same but *that* shows how we're different from each other really.

JACK. I think I popped out –

BEA. Jack-in-the-box –

JACK. And Bea was crying so much that I thought *that* was *her* job.

BEA. Sophie, Jack never cries. I'm the crybaby, he's the mouse. Jack-is-a-mouse-in-a-box.

JACK. I never cry about anything.

BEA. That's 'cos you're such a brainbox – Jack's-got-a-brain-in-a-box.

SOPHIE. Those are your parents' clothes, aren't they?

JACK. Do you remember what we do on our birthday?

SOPHIE. No.

JACK. Oh, come on, Sophie, it's a very simple thing that everybody does.

SOPHIE. I can't possibly imagine.

BEA. You're not even trying, Sophie.

SOPHIE. You're right, I'm not. Why are you both wearing your parents' clothes again?

JACK. First things first and I'll give you a clue –

BEA. Oh, it's so easy! Everyone does it, but we do it a little bit different, remember?

JACK. Come on!

SOPHIE. Is this the only way I'm going to get any answers out of you?

JACK. It's all part of the day, Sophie.

BEA. Sophie!

SOPHIE. Oh God, I know it's your birthday, but I completely forgot.

BEA. It doesn't matter – what do you do on a birthday? Don't be such a thicko.

SOPHIE. I... I... I should be giving you a present, shouldn't I, is that what you're getting at?

JACK *and* BEA. Yes!

SOPHIE. I'm sorry, I don't have any. I forgot. I'm sorry.

JACK. Don't be sorry, Sophie. Don't worry about that.

BEA. But don't you remember what happens on birthdays in our family? How we do it different from everybody?

SOPHIE. No, no, I don't, I can't remember.

BEA. Really? You really don't remember?

JACK. I told you, I told you she wouldn't remember.

BEA. Didn't we do it even when we were little, when you were here before?

JACK. We'll just have to remind her about it.

BEA. I've never forgotten. I think it's happened for ever.

JACK. We give you a present too –

BEA. We give you a present *too*.

...

Not a big one, 'cos it's very important that the birthday boy and girl – that's us – or actually it could be Mum and Dad when it's their birthday – it's very important that they get the better present.

JACK. 'Cos it's their *actual* birthday on that day.

SOPHIE. But I don't have a present to give you. I... I could go and get something.

JACK. We've already got one and one from you to us –

BEA. Dad tells this joke that –

JACK. 'We deserve a bloody present for looking after you all year round.'

BEA. But actually it's 'cos Mum thinks –

JACK. That if you get given a gift –

BEA. 'Then a gift in return is the best form of thank-you.'

JACK. My mum is full of nice sentiments.

BEA. It doesn't have to be a proper present, but you've got to give something back. It could just be a kiss. That's the rule. But once you know the rule, then you're ready for it.

JACK. We're ready for it.

BEA. Ready ready ready –

JACK. Like rabbits rabbits rabbits –

SOPHIE. Do I get to see this present I'm to give you?

BEA. Oh, I don't know. I can't remember.

JACK. I don't think that will get in the way.

SOPHIE. Get in the way of what?

JACK. Of the day, of what's to do.

SOPHIE. What is there to do?

JACK. Oh, quite a lot.

BEA. Birthdays are busy days.

JACK. Yes, they are. We've got our foot on the gas.

BEA. Jack, Jack – can I go and get the presents?

JACK. Yes, I think so.

> BEA *runs out of the door.*
>
> ...
>
> BEA *re-enters.*

She holds two envelopes. One has 'Sophie' written on it. The other is bigger and has 'Jack and Bea' written on it. Both envelopes are unsealed.

BEA. Here we are – oh, I love it I love it I love it!

(*To* SOPHIE.) Here's your one.

JACK. Don't give her the wrong one.

BEA. I wrote the names on, didn't I?

JACK. Just be careful.

BEA. Chill out, brainbox. Here you are, Sophie.

BEA gives SOPHIE *the envelope with 'Jack and Bea' written on it.*

SOPHIE. Thank you.

BEA. No, that's not our present to you, it's the one you have to give us.

SOPHIE. Yes, yes, I know, I know.

JACK. Give me the other one, please.

BEA. I'll look after it. Look, I can put it down my dress, like Mum does when she hides things.

JACK. I think it's better to hide it like Dad does – inside my jacket pocket. Which is where I put my wallet and car keys too. It's the safest place.

BEA. Yeah, definitely.

BEA gives JACK *the envelope and he puts it inside his jacket pocket.*

Come on then, Sophie!

SOPHIE looks at the envelope in her hands.

SOPHIE. Is this what you're all dressed up for?

JACK. You've got to dress up on your birthday.

BEA. And to go on holiday too –

SOPHIE. But I told you I can't take you –

BEA. Oh, can we have our present now, please?

Oh, come on, Sophie – please!

SOPHIE *goes to give it as* BEA *steps forward to take it. Just before* BEA *grabs it,* SOPHIE *turns around and opens the envelope to have a look.*

Oi!

SOPHIE. I just want to see what I'm giving you, that's all.

SOPHIE *opens the envelope and takes out a photo. She has never seen this photo before. It freezes her to the spot.*

BEA. Come on then.

Sophie?

JACK. Come on, Sophie.

SOPHIE. Why are you giving this to me?

BEA. We're not, silly, I just told you, it's for us, isn't it – it's the present from you to us.

JACK. I really like it. It's a really nice photo, I think.

SOPHIE. Where is this photo from?

JACK. We found it upstairs last night.

BEA. We knew we had to find some presents, and we couldn't go and get any, obviously we can't drive the car yet, and it was the middle of the night –

JACK. We don't have a car any more, but we will when we go on holiday, won't we, Sophie – ?

BEA. Oh yeah, course –

SOPHIE. Of course you will, Jack –

JACK. You have to sit in the back seat, Sophie.

BEA. Yeah!

SOPHIE. How wonderful, that's where I usually sit – where did you get this photo from?

BEA. We had a look through all the rooms and then we found this shoebox in the study with all this stuff in it, but also there were these photos.

JACK. I thought that would be the best present.

BEA. I think you look really pretty in it. I really like it, 'cos Mum and Dad and you are all in it together wearing birthday hats and I'd never seen a photo of you with Mum and Dad before.

JACK. I thought they'd be dusty, but they weren't that dusty.

BEA. I really like that one. We're going to keep it for good luck.

Can we have it now?

JACK. Can we have it now, please, Sophie?

...

SOPHIE. And what are you going to give me?

JACK. Oh, come on, Sophie, that's a surprise.

BEA. Yeah, and anyway, you have to give us our present first, 'cos it's our birthday.

BEA *moves over to* SOPHIE.

SOPHIE *puts the photo in the envelope and gives it to* BEA.

Thank you very much for my lovely birthday gift, Sophie.

BEA *kisses* SOPHIE *lightly on the lips, then walks to* JACK *and gives him the card.*

JACK *walks over to* SOPHIE.

JACK. Thank you very much for my lovely birthday gift, Sophie.

JACK *kisses* SOPHIE *lightly on the lips. He then walks back towards* BEA, *opening the envelope and looking at the photo again.*

You do look very pretty in it.

SOPHIE. Why would you want a photo of me with your mother and father?

BEA. We want to remember you.

> JACK *puts the photo* SOPHIE *has just given them back in his pocket.*

SOPHIE. What's my gift? Is it another photo?

BEA. We're not going to tell you, are we? No way!

SOPHIE. It is, isn't it?

BEA. We're not going to tell you before we give it to you –

SOPHIE. Can I have it now?

BEA. Jack, where have you put it?

JACK. It's in my pocket, silly.

BEA. Let me give it to Sophie.

JACK. No, not yet.

SOPHIE. I'd really like to see it.

JACK. BeaBea, we've got to get everything right first, remember?

BEA. Oh, yeah, course, sorry. I got carried away with it all.

SOPHIE. Jack, can I have a look at that photo, please?

JACK. Who said it was a photo?

SOPHIE. Stop playing silly buggers with me – please just pass it over.

BEA. Jack, you're a silly bugger!

JACK. Sophie, why are you getting angry?

SOPHIE. I'm not getting angry, I'd just like to see the photo.

BEA. Who said it was a photo, Sophie?

SOPHIE. You said there were *photos* – you said *photos*.

BEA. Sophie, stop it, you're spoiling the fun. First, we've got to get everything right before we give you the present. It's your birthday-holiday present. It's your going-away present. We've got to make it all special first.

SOPHIE. Why? What's so special about it?

JACK. It's a special day – it's our special day.

BEA. I think Jack looks as swish-as-a-dish.

JACK. I do not.

BEA. Yeah, you do. All the girls fancy you.

JACK. Shut up.

BEA. What d'you think, Sophie?

JACK. Don't ask her, what does she know?

BEA. Don't you think Jack looks swish-as-a-dish in his suit?

SOPHIE. Jack looks just –

BEA. It's one of Daddy's special party suits.

JACK. And my party tie.

SOPHIE. And you look –

BEA. This is one of Mummy's party dresses. I don't think
they'll mind us wearing them.

JACK. We don't mind. I think that we have to put things to their
proper use.

BEA. Dad says that.

SOPHIE. Isn't it a little early for a party?

BEA. Oh, don't worry, we've got it all ready. I know all the
things that we need and I did them all last night. I haven't
been to sleep or anything.

JACK. I said we could do it in the morning.

BEA. I stayed up all night long to get it all done. It was brilliant.

JACK. But we still have to do the decorations and pack the car.

BEA. Yeah, I didn't do that, Sophie, 'cos I didn't want to wake
you up –

SOPHIE. Pack the car – ?

JACK. It's raining today, Bea.

BEA. What? Oh no!

JACK. We'll have to drive safely, but maybe it will clear up.

BEA. It has to.

JACK. I'm sure it will, darling.

BEA. The first thing to do is get your party clothes on.

SOPHIE. What?

BEA. We're all dressed up so you have to too.

SOPHIE. This is ridiculous, it's probably only nine o'clock in the morning.

BEA. Don't you want your present, Sophie?

If you want your present, you have to get dressed up and join in. It's important, don't you see?

SOPHIE. I don't have any party clothes with me – I don't even own any *party clothes* –

JACK. Oh, don't worry about that.

BEA. Yeah, don't worry, I've made you some things to wear.

SOPHIE. You've made something?

BEA. Yeah, I think you'll like it. It's pretty silly but it's very important.

JACK. You're going to look pretty silly, Sophie.

BEA. Yeah, but it's a party so it's okay to look silly. Don't let Jack tease you. He knows nothing about fashion, remember? Oh, it's brilliant, we've got birthday hats and everything.

BEA *runs out.*

...

BEA *runs back in with a bag full of clothes.*

Jack, Jack, do you want to do the rest now?

JACK. Yes, I think we're ready.

BEA. Yeah!

> JACK *runs out.*

> Sophie, Sophie, here you go. Ready?

SOPHIE. Bea, where's Jack gone?

BEA. He's just getting the decorations – right, first is your skirt.

> BEA *pulls out a skirt. It is made up of two of* BEA*'s skirts sewn very basically together, as if she cut each one to open them up and then made one larger skirt. Both are simple primary-coloured skirts.*

> Ta-dah! What do you think? Do you see what I did? I got two of my skirts and sewed them together so it would fit you properly.

> JACK *quietly re-enters holding a bunch of withered white and red roses and a pile of cards. He immediately starts to move about the room carefully distributing the flowers and the cards. It should eventually become clear that the cards and roses are from Philip & Ros's funeral.*

> Put it on, put it on! I don't mind if you put it on over your other skirt.

SOPHIE. Bea…

BEA. Please, Sophie, please!

> SOPHIE *puts on the skirt over the one she's currently wearing.*

> Oh, that looks brilliant. Doesn't it, Jack?

JACK. Hang on.

BEA. Jack's bit next – I had to make it though, 'cos Jack can't sew.

> BEA *pulls out a light blue T-shirt. On it is a basically sewn segment of T-shirt fabric that has been cut out of another T-shirt. The segment has printed on it, in large, childish blue letters, the name 'Jack'.*

> I got one of Dad's big T-shirts and sewed on Jack's name from his T-shirt from when he was a little boy. Do you remember it?

SOPHIE. No.

BEA. It was Jack's favourite T-shirt but he can't wear it any
more because he's a big boy now. Don't worry, he didn't
mind me cutting it out.

JACK. I don't mind.

BEA. Go on, put it on.

SOPHIE *puts the T-shirt on.*

Doesn't she look brilliant?

JACK. She looks like you and me put together.

BEA. And I've got my fairy wings for you to wear, 'cos you're
a guardian angel.

BEA *takes the last items out of the bag: some small toy fairy
wings that clip onto clothing*

Sophie, turn round, please.

SOPHIE *does so. As she does, she takes in* JACK*'s handi-
work: the room is now very lightly scattered with roses and
cards.*

SOPHIE. Oh…

BEA *clips the fairy wings onto the back of the T-shirt.*

BEA. Brilliant!

JACK. I think that's sufficient.

BEA. Oh, look – that's brilliant – birthday cards and flowers!

SOPHIE *turns back around.*

SOPHIE. Jack, why have you put those – ?

BEA. Oh no, I've forgot the birthday hats –

BEA *delves into the bag and pulls out three Christmas
crackers.*

SOPHIE. Jack – ?

BEA. I could only find Christmas crackers. They have hats in them, don't they? Jack, come here – we need to pull them all together at the same time.

BEA hands them a Christmas cracker each. JACK and BEA cross their arms over, like at Christmas dinner, and take the opposite cracker to pull.

SOPHIE. Jack, those flowers, those roses –

JACK. They're just decorations for the party – don't you think they're pretty?

BEA. Really pretty. Come on, Sophie, take my cracker –

SOPHIE. Look, no, that's not right, it's not… proper, don't you understand?

JACK. Why? I think they're all very evenly distributed, aren't they, BeaBea?

BEA. Yeah, you could be a flower arranger when you grow up.

JACK. Shut up.

BEA. Oh, come on, Sophie, we can't start without you.

SOPHIE looks down at her Christmas cracker and around at the flowers and cards.

Sophie?

Come on, we have to have birthday hats for the party.

SOPHIE takes hold of two crackers, crossing over her arms like JACK and BEA.

Ready? One, two – actually, I've got an idea – the pop of the crackers is the official start of the party – like cutting a ribbon or something.

JACK. Or smashing a bottle on a ship.

BEA. Yeah!

Ready? One… two… three!

They pull. The crackers pop open. JACK and BEA cheer.

BEA *gives* JACK *a kiss, then* SOPHIE *too.*

Three paper party hats (in the shape of crowns) fall on the floor.

BEA *and* JACK *pick up the hats.* BEA *gives a hat to* SOPHIE.

There you go, Sophie.

JACK *and* BEA *put on their hats.* SOPHIE *hesitates.*

Sophie?

You've got to put your hat on, it's important.

BEA *puts the hat on* SOPHIE*'s head.*

Jack, go and get the food and the squash. Quick!

JACK. I will, darling.

BEA. Thank you, darling.

JACK *exits.*

We've got sausage rolls and everything, just like before.

SOPHIE. When?

BEA. What?

SOPHIE. When did you have them before?

BEA. Oh, you know, just a few days ago, at the going-away party, at the goodbye party. There was loads left over in the fridge.

SOPHIE. You mean the funeral, the reception after the funeral?

BEA. There was loads left over on trays in the fridge which we didn't take.

JACK *enters with a tray. On it are a jug of squash, two glasses filled with squash, one empty glass, a big bowl of small sausage rolls, and some paper party plates.*

JACK. I couldn't fit the cake on the tray.

BEA. Jack!

JACK. Oh, sorry.

BEA. It was supposed to be a surprise!

JACK. I know. Sorry, I didn't think right.

BEA. You're such an idiot.

JACK. I'm sure we can still enjoy it just as much as before.

BEA. I doubt it.

JACK. I didn't mean to. Please don't let it spoil the party, darling.

BEA. I can't believe you told us about the cake.

JACK. I didn't mean to.

BEA. I know, but still!

JACK. Let's not have a big argument.

  Do you forgive me, darling?

BEA. You're such an idiot.

JACK (*to* SOPHIE). Do you want a glass of squash?

BEA. Sophie, can you forget you heard about the cake? Can we make it still like a surprise? Just for me?

SOPHIE. If you want.

JACK. Cake? What cake?

BEA. Yeah, what cake?

  (*To* SOPHIE.) Do you want a glass of squash and a sausage roll?

SOPHIE. No thank you.

BEA. But you've got to – it's a party.

SOPHIE. I'm not hungry.

BEA. But it's your party too.

JACK. Yes, it's your party too.

SOPHIE. I couldn't, I'm not hungry.

  JACK *puts some sausage rolls on a plate and pours a glass of squash from the jug.*

BEA. Oh, go on, just the one.

SOPHIE. I said, no thank you.

BEA. Jack's going to eat about a thousand.

JACK. I'm a greedy pig.

BEA. He'll eat all of yours if you're not careful.

SOPHIE. He's welcome to them.

> JACK *walks to* SOPHIE *and puts the plate of sausage rolls and big glass of squash in front of her.*

JACK. There you go.

SOPHIE. I just said I don't want any.

JACK. Don't you even want your squash?

SOPHIE. No, I don't, thank you.

JACK. Breakfast is the most important meal of the day.

SOPHIE. I don't mean to be spoiling the party, but I just don't want to eat sausage rolls at nine o'clock in the morning.

JACK. If you don't eat your greens you'll get no dessert.

BEA. Uh oh...

SOPHIE. I beg your pardon? What did you just say?

JACK. You'll be grateful for what you've got, young lady, and if you expect to get a birthday present today, you'll eat what's in front of you.

BEA. That's brilliant!

JACK. Thank you, darling.

> JACK *takes out the photo again and looks at it.*

BEA (*to* SOPHIE). Remember we've still got to give you your present, but only after the food and cake. Whoops! Aaarrgh! Forget the cake – forget I said about the cake.

JACK. We're almost finished, aren't we?

BEA. Yeah, I thought there were so many pieces, but there aren't that many actually.

JACK. I get all tingly looking at this photo, but now everyone's here together, like before.

BEA (*to* SOPHIE). When was that photo?

SOPHIE. I can't remember.

BEA. Was it on the shouting birthday?

SOPHIE. It might have been.

BEA. You're very pretty in it. I bet you had loads of boyfriends.

SOPHIE. Boyfriends?

BEA. Yeah – did you?

SOPHIE. I don't… I – I didn't, no, not really.

BEA. Oh, come on, Sophie, how many? How many did you have?

SOPHIE. I…

BEA. Who's your boyfriend now?

SOPHIE. I don't have a boyfriend at the moment –

BEA. Why?

JACK. Everyone's smiling, very happily. They're looking at the camera, but you're not –

BEA. Oh, yeah –

JACK. You're looking at Mummy and Daddy, like you're… looking for something. I like that. I know that feeling.

BEA. That's 'cos you're a nosy parker.

JACK eats a sausage roll.

And a greedy pig.

JACK hands BEA one of the pre-poured glasses of squash. He takes the other one.

Thank you, darling.

JACK. My pleasure, darling. Down the hatch.

BEA. What, all at once?

JACK. That's the spirit.

BEA. What if I get pukey?

JACK. We'll do it together, with Sophie.

BEA. Oh, yeah.

JACK. Never fear, Dad is here.

BEA. Only if we do it together with Sophie. Sophie?

SOPHIE. What?

JACK. Down the hatch, all together, in one gulp.

SOPHIE. Why on earth do you want to do that?

JACK. It's a challenge, it's a party game.

BEA. Yeah, who can gulp it the quickest –

JACK. That's right, we're usually the quickest, so you'll
    probably win.

SOPHIE. For God's sake…

BEA. Please, Sophie, don't spoil the party, if you don't play we
    can't begin.

SOPHIE. Bea…

BEA. Please.

JACK (*raising his glass*). Cheers!

BEA (*raising her glass*). Cheers!

    Sophie?

    SOPHIE *looks out at the rain, then she picks up her squash.*

JACK *and* BEA. Cheers!

    They all down their squash, JACK *and* BEA *hesitating only
    until* SOPHIE *begins to drink too.*

    JACK *and* BEA *share a glance as* SOPHIE *does so.*

    SOPHIE *gags in disgust.*

SOPHIE. Oh Christ – my God – what was that?

JACK. Just birthday squash. / Don't you like it? Is it too strong?

SOPHIE. Jesus – water – Bea, get me some water –

BEA, *shocked, dashes from the room.*

SOPHIE *coughs and gags again.*

How can you drink that?

JACK. We like it strong.

SOPHIE. It's disgusting –

JACK. Sorry / about that –

SOPHIE. Christ –

JACK. Sorry –

SOPHIE. Oh Jesus, I think I might be sick...

BEA *rushes back in with water.*

BEA. Here you are here you are.

BEA *gives* SOPHIE *the water. She takes a large gulp.*

SOPHIE *sits down.*

SOPHIE *feels increasingly light-headed and dizzy as the scene continues.*

Are you feeling ill, Sophie?

SOPHIE. I feel...

I feel a bit better... I don't know how you can stomach –

JACK. Do you want some cake?

SOPHIE. Absolutely not.

BEA. Can we bring it in though?

JACK. I'll get it.

JACK *exits.*

BEA. Sorry, Sophie.

SOPHIE. For what?

BEA. The squash. Sorry about it. Sorry.

SOPHIE. I can't believe you can drink it so strong.

BEA. Yeah…

   Do you feel really ill?

SOPHIE. No, just a little light-headed.

BEA. Oh good. That's good.

   Do you want some more water?

SOPHIE. I'm fine.

BEA. Will you still sing 'Happy Birthday'?

JACK (*from outside the door*). Are the lights all off?

BEA. Oh! Wait wait!

   BEA *rushes to the garden door and pulls a curtain across it.*
   The room is immediately thrown into darkness.

   Done it done it!

JACK. Ready?

BEA. Yeah!

JACK. Shut up!

BEA. Oops, sorry.

   The door opens. JACK *stands in the doorway with a*
   candlelit cake. It shouldn't become clear until the curtain is
   opened again, but it is a white-icing fruitcake from the
   funeral: it has a black ribbon around it and slices already
   missing.

   As JACK *walks into the room, he starts to sing.*

JACK. Happy Birthday to you…

JACK *and* BEA. Happy Birthday to you,
      Happy Birthday Jack and Bea,
      Happy Birthday to you.

   JACK *puts the cake down.*

JACK (*to* SOPHIE). Ready?

SOPHIE. What?

JACK. You've got to blow the candles out.

BEA. Yeah, go on, Sophie.

SOPHIE. But it's your birthday cake.

JACK. It's yours too –

BEA. Then you get your present.

JACK. Come on.

SOPHIE. Don't you want to?

JACK. It doesn't matter about that. It's important that you blow them out so everything is done properly. It's all part of the day.

BEA. It's all part of the *birth*day.

JACK. Yes, that's right.

SOPHIE. You've planned all this out, haven't you?

BEA. Yeah, course, we do it every birthday.

JACK. We're the little conspirators, remember?

BEA. Are we?

JACK. That's what we're called.

BEA. Oh, I like it, I like that name – like we're superheroes or something.

SOPHIE. And then what happens – after I blow out the candles and we eat the cake – ?

BEA. We give you your present –

SOPHIE. And then what? (*She is hit by wave of nausea.*) Oh Jesus…

BEA. What's wrong?

SOPHIE. Can you let some light in, please?

JACK. Blow the candles out first.

SOPHIE. Pull back the curtain.

Please.

BEA. Jack?

JACK. Blow out the candles first.

SOPHIE. Jesus Christ, Jack!

SOPHIE *blows out the candles. The room is once again plunged into gloom.*

SOPHIE *tries to get up, but sits back down. She groans.*

BEA. Sophie?

Sophie, are you alright?

Jack?

JACK. She'll be alright. Her tummy doesn't like squash, that's all.

BEA. Jack...

Sophie? Are you alright?

SOPHIE. I don't know...

BEA. Do you still feel as bad as just now?

JACK. She'll be fine and dandy, don't worry.

BEA. I am worried – I thought –

JACK. Sophie, you'll be right as rain, won't you?

SOPHIE. I feel dizzy, Bea, that's all.

BEA. Oh...

That's not so bad.

SOPHIE. Please open the curtains.

BEA *pulls back the curtain. The rain has stopped and the sky has cleared. Sunlight pours into the room.*

BEA. Look. Jack, look.

JACK. Brilliant.

I thought it would. I knew it.

(*Singing*.) The sun has got his hat on...

JACK *and* BEA. Hip hip hip hooray,
    The sun has got his hat on
    And we're going out to play.

JACK *takes the envelope marked 'Sophie' out of his pocket.*

JACK. I hope you like it.

JACK *gives* SOPHIE *the envelope. She stares at it, her head swimming.*

...

Aren't you going to open it?

It's from us.

BEA. With love.

JACK. Yes, with love from us to you.

SOPHIE *opens the envelope and takes out a photo. She stares at it.*

...

SOPHIE. Oh God...

BEA. What's wrong? Don't you like it?

SOPHIE. This was... with the other photo?

BEA. Yeah.

SOPHIE. Was there... anything else?

BEA. Anything else?

SOPHIE. With the... photos.

BEA. Just bits of paper and stuff.

SOPHIE. Paper?

BEA. Yeah.

SOPHIE. What paper?

BEA. I dunno, I didn't really look, it was all folded up. I just saw the photos. Sophie, are you okay?

I think you look more beautiful in that one than our one. Are you younger in this one? Is it from before the other photo?

What's wrong? Don't you like it? Are you still feeling ill?

SOPHIE. Where are they?

BEA. What?

SOPHIE. The papers.

BEA. Upstairs. In the box. Jack had it.

Jack?

JACK. It doesn't matter.

BEA. Oh.

...

SOPHIE. Are they...? Did you read...?

JACK. It doesn't matter any more. Don't you like the photo?

I like it very much indeed.

SOPHIE. Did you read / those – ?

JACK. You look younger than in the other photo. Definitely.

SOPHIE. Oh Jesus –

BEA. What's wrong, Sophie? Why are you crying?

JACK (*still referring to the photo*). Who took it?

SOPHIE. Stop it –

BEA. Don't cry, Sophie, don't cry.

SOPHIE. Please tell me / you didn't...

BEA. What's wrong, Sophie?

Jack, what is it? What's going on?

JACK. It doesn't matter about them any more. It's not important any more.

SOPHIE. I'm sorry...

BEA. What are the papers?

JACK. It doesn't matter.

BEA. Tell me.

JACK. It doesn't matter.

BEA. Tell me!

...

JACK. They're just letters.

BEA. Oh.

Who wrote them?

Who wrote them?

JACK. Sophie did.

BEA. Why? What, to Mummy and Daddy?

JACK. No.

BEA. To Mummy?

JACK. No.

BEA. What, to Daddy?

Sophie wrote them to Daddy?

JACK. Yes.

BEA. What do they say?

Jack, what do they say?

JACK. Just silly things, it doesn't matter –

BEA. What things?

JACK. Just silly, stupid – 'Forgive me, forget me, / love
Sophie – '

SOPHIE. Jack –

BEA. I don't understand – why's Sophie crying about it?

JACK. It doesn't matter – it's stupid – let's get on with the party – we're nearly finished and then it's time to go away.

BEA. I know, I know that, I'm not an idiot – I want to know why Sophie's crying about it –

JACK. Bea –

BEA. Don't treat me like a baby – what else do they say? – I'm not a baby –

JACK. I know –

BEA. Then tell me!

I can go and read them myself, you know. I know where they are, you know.

JACK. Sophie loved Daddy and Daddy loved Sophie.

SOPHIE. Oh God...

JACK. That's what the letters say.

That's all.

Over and over again.

BEA. Oh.

SOPHIE. I'm so sorry...

JACK. Why? That doesn't matter – not now we're going on holiday, not now it's the mourning, not now it's our birthday –

BEA. Sophie, did you love my daddy – ?

JACK. That's not important, that doesn't matter! It's all here together right now and then once we finish it's the holiday, it's the going away – and then we can come home and start again –

SOPHIE. I'm sorry, Bea... –

BEA. I don't understand. Why? What about Mummy?

JACK. BeaBea –

BEA. What about Mummy? Didn't Daddy love Mummy?

JACK. But BeaBea, we're nearly finished and then we can –

BEA. Yes, but does that mean that Daddy didn't love –

JACK. It doesn't… it doesn't change those things we talked ᵉabout, BeaBea – it's all still the same – isn't it? Sophie will fall asleep soon, like she's us, like she's us in the car, and then we go away like Mum and Dad, because it's the holiday, remember? It's important we do it today, remember? It's our birthday. It hasn't changed the things that need to be done. We've still got to pick up all the pieces, BeaBea.

BeaBea?

SOPHIE *tries to get up, but is overcome by dizziness and nausea.*

SOPHIE *puts her hand over her mouth, to stop vomiting. She holds it back.*

BEA. Sophie? Jack, you said she'd be alright – you said she'd be alright, Jack –

JACK. She will be alright – she'll just go to sleep, that's all – don't panic / about it.

SOPHIE. Jack… Jack… / What have you…?

BEA. Jack, stop it – make Sophie better –

JACK. Don't worry about it, don't worry about it –

SOPHIE *again chokes back vomit.*

BEA. Jack!

JACK. Don't worry about it – she'll just go to sleep, that's all – / that's all –

BEA. How many did you put in? Why's Sophie got so ill? Jack!

JACK (*shouting*). Don't shout! –

BEA. Stop it! –

JACK. Don't shout don't shout!

SOPHIE *vomits onto herself a small amount.*

BEA *starts to cry.*

BEA. No!

SOPHIE. Help me…

JACK. I didn't put many in, BeaBea – only a few – she's only supposed to go to sleep –

BEA. Stop it stop it – I hate it I hate it / I hate it!

JACK. BeaBea, don't shout – please – she'll just go to sleep that's all – that's all –

BEA. No!

SOPHIE. Jack…

SOPHIE *slumps forward.*

JACK. She'll only go to sleep, BeaBea – I didn't put that many in – really – I promise – I promise you.

You're only going to go to sleep, Sophie. Just for a bit. That's what they do. It said so on the label. Don't worry.

BEA. I want my mummy…

JACK. No…

BEA. I do I do. I want my mummy here right now.

JACK. No, BeaBea, no.

BEA. Yes!

JACK. But she can't! That's what we've got to do, BeaBea, we've got to do all those things – you do what Mum does, and I do what Dad does, remember?

BEA. I don't want to any more, I just want Mummy and Daddy back –

JACK. We have to pick up the pieces – we have to get back to work – we have to pick ourselves up.

That's what we have to do – everything says so. Everything.

BEA. No…

> JACK *holds* BEA.

> SOPHIE *falls to one side. She is still clutching the photo. She is barely conscious.*

> JACK *and* BEA *look at her.*

Sophie?

SOPHIE. Ros…

JACK. Sophie?

SOPHIE. Philip…

> …

JACK. She's just going to sleep.

> It said so on the label.

BEA. Okay.

> …

JACK. It's time to go now, I think.

BEA. Will Sophie be alright?

JACK. It said so on the label.

> …

BEA. Jack?

JACK. Let's go.

> JACK *walks over to the suitcases, picks them up and brings them back to* BEA.

BEA. Wait. Don't we have to pack the car?

JACK. Oh, I forgot.

> *They look at* SOPHIE *for a moment and then they look around.*

BEA. I know.

BEA *walks to a pile of books and lifts them carefully over to the sofa where* SOPHIE *is slumped.* BEA *gently lays them down next to* SOPHIE.

Slowly, methodically, JACK *and* BEA *surround* SOPHIE *with books, until she is securely packed into the sofa.*

They walk back to their suitcases.

BEA *walks over to* SOPHIE, *bends down and kisses her on her head.*

Bye bye, sleep tight, mind the bedbugs don't bite.

JACK. Do her seatbelt up.

BEA *does this.*

BEA *walks back to* JACK.

BEA. Jack?

JACK. Yes?

BEA. Where are we going to go?

JACK. I don't know.

Somewhere.

Home.

JACK *walks over to* SOPHIE *and kisses her on the head.*

JACK *walks back to* BEA. *They pick up their suitcases.*

They take each other's hand and walk to the garden door.

They open it.

Sunlight pours in.

They pause a moment.

They walk out into the sun.

The End.

Acknowledgements

I would like to thank for their help, inspiration, encouragement or trust, in order of earliest to most recent acquaintance, my parents Robert and Philippa, my brothers Llewellyn, Cennydd and Aled, Amy Hodge, Roger Mortimer, Simon Appleton, Alasdair Middleton, Ben Woolf and MyAnna Buring (and everyone associated with MahWaff Theatre Company), Kate Wasserberg and all the team at Clwyd Theatr Cymru, and Lily Williams.

H.J.

A Nick Hern Book

Pieces first published in Great Britain as a paperback original in 2010 by
Nick Hern Books, 14 Larden Road, London W3 7ST, in association with
Clwyd Theatr Cymru

Pieces copyright © 2010 Hywel John

Hywel John has asserted his right to be identified as the author of this work

Cover image by Dewynters
Cover designed by Ned Hoste, 2H

Typeset by Nick Hern Books, London
Printed in the UK by CLE Print Ltd, St Ives, Cambs, PE27 3LE

A CIP catalogue record for this book is available from the British Library

ISBN   978 1 84842 111 0